COMMUNISM TODAY

Other works by Douglas Hyde:

The Answer to Communism, 1949.
I Believed, 1950.
Red Star versus the Cross (with Francis Dufay), 1954.
One Front across the World, 1955.
The Mind behind New China, 1956.
God's Bandit, 1957.
Communism in Asia, 1960.
The Peaceful Assault, 1963.
United We Fall, 1964.
Confrontation in the East, 1965.
Dedication and Leadership: Learning from the Communists, 1966.
He who Rides the Tiger (with Luis Taruc), 1967.
The Troubled Continent: a New Look at Latin America, 1967.
The Roots of Guerrilla Warfare, 1968.

COMMUNISM TODAY

DOUGLAS HYDE

UNIVERSITY OF NOTRE DAME PRESS

American edition 1973

UNIVERSITY OF NOTRE DAME PRESS

Notre Dame, Indiana 46556

First published 1972 by

Gill and Macmillan Limited
2 Belvedere Place
Dublin 1
Ireland
and in London through association with the
Macmillan
Group of Publishing Companies

Library of Congress Cataloging in Publication Data

Hyde, Douglas Arnold, 1911–
        Communism today

        Includes bibliographies
        1. Communism   2. Communism– 1945–   I. Title.
HX40.H88   335.43   72–12639
ISBN 0–268–00491–9
ISBN 0–268–00493–5   (pbk)

Printed and bound in the Republic of Ireland by
The Richview Press Limited, Dublin

TO ROSEMARY

who typed, checked and devotedly worked on this book,
and to whom a dedication was long overdue

Contents

Contents

Introduction

'TAKE a look at your book and see if it needs to be brought up to date,' a university lecturer suggested to me. He and his students had been using it for nearly twenty years but now it was out of print. 'We would be glad to see it republished,' he said.

The book was one I had written soon after I left the Communist Party to become a Catholic in 1948. Symbolically it was published on May Day the following year. It was called 'The Answer to Communism'. Who but a very new convert would give it a title as resounding and unequivocal as that?

Now, after many years, I looked at the book again. I took it with me to read on a train journey thinking that I would put a question mark by any passage which might require rewriting, a cross by any which I would have to lose entirely. I finished it as I reached my destination. By then there were queries or crosses on every page. I knew there could be no question of just rewriting a paragraph here and there. The world and Communism along with it had changed so much in twenty years that what was needed was a new book. This is it.

For years as I travelled about the world I had been talking and writing about the changes which were occurring in the international scene. I had insisted that the world of Stalin, John Foster Dulles and Pius XII was not today's world. That one was characterised by its division into two mutually hostile camps, a black or white situation with all the 'goodies' allegedly in one camp and the 'baddies' in the other. Who were the 'goodies' and who the 'baddies' depended upon which camp you happened to be in yourself. Any attempt at neutralism was seen as some form of betrayal.

Today's world is characterised by its increasing fluidity. Where there was confrontation there is growing dialogue. There are by now people in both groups who acknowledge that they have not the whole truth, that the search for truth will continue throughout the ages, and who are willing to learn from each other. They recognise that even though their differences are fundamental both are in good faith and this at least they have in common. This is a more civilised and, if the Communists will pardon the expression, a more Christian attitude than the earlier one.

The change came, not simply because the main actors of the earlier period had moved off the stage, but because there had been a qualitative change in the world situation. Communists and Christians alike are continuing to react to it. Of course this does not apply to all Communists, nor yet to all Christians. There are some members of both groups who cling to the view that any change is a betrayal, regardless of what may be happening around them.

Stalinists survive as minority groups within the Communist parties of the West and their influence is very much alive at the topmost levels of government in the Soviet Union. Christian circles, too, have their 'Stalinists' to whom the new trends are anathema even though the World Council of Churches and the Catholic Church—as much under Paul VI as under John XXIII—have shown themselves ready to explore and where necessary to initiate Christian-Marxist dialogue as part of a broader movement towards the new openness. There are Western politicians and parties who have yet to adjust their minds to what has happened. The old black or white situation was so much easier to understand, so much simpler to present to others, and so very much better as a basis for rewarding campaigns and crusades. More significant, however, is the immense distance travelled by those who have responded to the changing needs and opportunities created by a rapidly changing situation without any betrayal of integrity on the part of either.

To a striking extent it has been identical developments in the world situation which have brought about the changed attitudes of the two groups. Let me outline just three of these which come most readily to mind.

1. *The threat of annihilation.* It took some years for the full significance of what it means to live in a nuclear age to sink in. But as the consequences of man's new-found ability to destroy all life on earth, meaning among other things the end of both capitalism and Communism, became clear so too did something else. This was most aptly expressed by Roger Garaudy, at that time a member of the Political Bureau of the French Communist Party. Urging the need for Christian-Marxist dialogue he wrote that 'a crusade between two confronting dogmatisms in the present state of technique of

destruction means the annihilation of mankind.' It was not only Christians, of course, who had been confronting the Communist 'dogmatism' with their own. Many politicians and idealogues had been doing the same.

For the best of pragmatic reasons, therefore, quite apart from those of principle, neither side could do anything but recoil from the possibility of a war of annihilation. The search for peace, the need to find a way to co-exist, became a matter of survival, But for each, to get away from the concept of crusading against the other meant that some very new thinking was going to be urgently required and a lot of prejudices would have to be shed.

It will be observed that in thus making my point I have put Communism on one 'side' and both capitalism and Christianity alike on the other. The fact is that at that time institutional Christianity tended most often to be ranged on the side of what was euphemistically called 'the West' in the East-West conflict. Today the World Council of Churches has already largely extricated itself from that situation and the Vatican under Pope Paul's leadership would appear also to be pursuing a policy of disengagement and aiming at a position where it can talk to both sides. This does not mean that either side is under any obligation to depart from its own fundamental beliefs.

Over and above the recognition of the new needs created by the coming of the nuclear age was a growing conviction on both sides of the existing gulf that if they went on thinking, talking and behaving in the old way they would at the very best themselves become increasingly irrelevant. This was thus a situation which called for some pretty drastic up-dating, renewal—'aggiornamento'.

2. *The new affluence.* Then there were, too, the new pro-

blems raised by the increasing and unprecedented affluence which science and technology were bringing to people in the most advanced countries of both camps. Among the Communists the emphasis had until then been upon the masses, whereas the emphasis on the other side had been on the individual. This was understandable.

Individualism had been the bedrock on which capitalism had been built, and Christians had, in theory at least, traditionally upheld the sanctity of the individual against threats from any quarter. The individual versus collectivism was therefore part of the overall picture of East-West confrontation.

In the Soviet Union an unprecedented attempt was being made to change in the shortest possible time the whole way of life of millions. Everything was subordinated to the Herculean task of destroying an old, unjust system and laying the foundations for a better one. Doctrine apart, it was almost inevitable that the emphasis should be on the role of the masses. To them everything had to be subordinated including the individual, his rights and problems.

In the Communist parties of the non-Communist world the stress was similarly on the masses. For from their inception they had believed that the early collapse of capitalism was within the range of possibilities, and the masses were the instrument of revolutionary change. It is, in any case, normal for revolutionary organisations to take the view that it is the cause, not the individual, that counts when revolution is on the agenda.

So problems of the individual were regarded as of secondary significance, the more so because, since they had their roots in the old system, they must necessarily await solution pending the building of the new one.

However, by the time the thaw in the cold war came

perspectives had changed for Communists in both camps. In Russia the foundations of socialism and of a modern technological society had now been laid. Belts had no longer to be pulled in so tightly and the rising standard of life was beginning to make its impact on people's attitudes. Communist parties on both sides of the iron curtain found that as living standards went up missionary fervour tended to go down. Even revolutionaries tended to become more relaxed. It is a problem not unknown to Christians.

Affluence, not the looked-for revolution, had come to the capitalist countries of the West. As the revolution receded over the horizon, party members themselves had time and opportunity to become for the first time concerned about their own and others' personal problems. Moreover, the growth of affluence and the speed of change brought new and pressing problems to the public whom they were trying to influence. These were not so much directly economic (as had been the case in the twenties and thirties) but psychological. They concerned the quality of life in the here and now, not in some more ideal society of the future. Western sociologists found themselves absorbed in new studies and increasingly engaged in a search for answers to the problems of adjustment which crowded in upon them from all sides.

Common to both the socialist and the capitalist countries was the growing problem—which assumed greater significance as the technological revolution proceeded—of the alienation of the individual from himself, his work, his fellows and the society in which he lived. He might have tens of thousands of work mates, live in some vast connurbation, yet feel isolated and alone, estranged from himself, a stranger in a strange land. He might have more gadgets in his home, more money in his pay packet—for what that was worth—yet feel that he had even less say in the decisions that determined his destiny than ever before. Psychiatric wards filled far more rapidly than did the ranks of the Communist Party.

All this led to the rediscovery of Marx's early and now highly relevant writings on alienation and a belated recognition that this had been a major concern of his all over the years driving him from philosophy into the field of economics and to half a life-time among the books in the British Museum in a search for answers to it.

Christians may be tempted to scoff at the new emphases in Communist thought today and at the delayed importance given to Marxist texts which had been there all the time had anyone bothered to publish them. They should perhaps reflect that this is not too unlike the recent and equally belated growth in recognition given to scripture scholars within the Catholic Church, the new interpretations and emphases placed on well-known texts and the importance accorded to some that were hitherto neglected but now found to be peculiarly relevant to our time.

What is certain is that if the growth of affluence has created headaches for Communists, the concomitant growth in materialism has done the same for Christians whose problems are remarkably similar.

3. *The impact of the Third World.* The emergence of scores of new, independent, developing, thrusting countries has transformed the world scene and compelled new thinking all round. It is not just the maps that have changed but the thinking of politicians, too, as they have had to consider and reconsider, for example, the purposes and consequences of aid to the Third World.

New trends of thought have come to both Communism and Christianity from, and been provoked by, developments

in Asia, Africa and Latin America. For the Communists there
are the progressive, anti-imperialist, military regimes of Latin
America, 'African socialism' which, though militant and
sympathetic to the socialist countries usually owes little to
Marx and nothing to atheism. For Christians there are the
young churches of the mission lands to disturb some fondly
held beliefs, challenge some of the old orthodoxies. For both
there has been the mind-expanding experience of coming to
understand the position of President Julius Nyerere of
Tanzania, a deeply committed Christian whose socialism falls
far short of being Marxist, yet whose credentials as an anti-
imperialist are impeccable. Similarly, to personalise again,
there is the challenge of the late Camilo Torres, guerrilla
leader and priest who symbolises one aspect of Latin American
revolutionary Christianity, with Archbishop Helder Camara,
every bit as revolutionary but with firmly held pacifist
principles, symbolising another.

Events and developments refuse any longer to conform to
old patterns, slot neatly into pre-conceived categories or recognise the need for iron curtains. A consequence is that anything
written fifteen years ago about Communism is as out of date
as anything written before Vatican II about the Catholic
Church. This is all the more so since numerous Marxist
thinkers have escaped from the straitjacket which Stalin
imposed upon Communist thought, yet still continue for as
long as they are able to speak from within the Communist
Party. Their eyes are wide open to the indisputable fact that,
since Marxism holds everything to be forever in a state of
flux and development, it should itself, contrary to recent
experience, be among the most open-ended of all beliefs.

Against this there are still among the Marxists, as among
the Christians, those who cling to the old-time religion which

'was good enough for Moses and it's good enough for me'.

This then is the background to this brief study of Communism as it is today with particular emphasis on the changes which have occurred and are still occurring in it.

1   Marxist-Leninist Origins

T<small>HE</small> Communist parties which exist in practically every country on earth today owe their origin and inspiration above all else to one man, Karl Marx. So, too, does the wider movement which in recent years has influenced increasing numbers of people who are not organised within the party yet have Communism as their aim.

Marx was of Jewish origin but to describe him as a German Jew and to leave it at that as so many have done can be misleading. His parents, in accord with a practice of the period, had become Protestants, largely, it is said, for social reasons. Be that as it may, if there was a certain lack of authenticity about the family's religious profession this no doubt played its part in ultimately prompting his revolt against religion. What is certain is that Marx was brought up as a Christian and that as a teenage boy, away at boarding school, he gave serious thought to his Christianity. It would seem from his letters to his father and from an essay which he wrote at the time that he did, in fact, have some sort of genuine religious experience.

Thus, even though in due course he totally rejected belief in God and the supernatural, two religious streams, Judaism and Christianity, contributed to his formation. His Judaic-Christian background possibly helps to explain why he seems always to have taken it for granted that an intelligent man should have strongly held beliefs and that these should be applied in practical fashion to the world about him. It may also have contributed to the strongly eschatological elements in his thinking and aspects of his Communist vision.

That his religious beliefs did not survive his first year at university need not surprise us. It would have been more surprising had they done so. As has been the case with many others, not least among his followers of today, he rejected the Christianity he observed. And who can blame him? For, born in 1818, he grew up at a time of outrageous exploitation and injustice. And, as often as not, the employers who exploited their workers most ferociously, loudly proclaimed their devotion to Christian principles. Over and above this, however, Marx's rejection of religion was an intellectual one. Most of the professors and nearly all his fellow students, first at Bonn then at Berlin, were caught up, as he soon was, in great philosophical battles in which atheism was pretty well taken for granted.

Then, as throughout his life, for Marx a battle of words was not enough. Words and action must go together. He was deeply concerned about men, their past trials, present plight, hopes for the future. Where others became armchair philosophers he became a political activist even whilst he was evolving his own philosophy. His was a turbulent, revolutionary period and he was committed to the idea of revolution even before he became a socialist.

For his social thinking there was already a growing body of socialist thought upon which to draw. There were French and German socialists, English Chartists, the Welshman, Robert Owen. He took what he wanted from each in turn.

James Connolly, the Irish nationalist and labour leader who was executed for his part in the Easter Rising in 1916, declared that he took his stand on scientific socialism as taught by Karl Marx. But he nonetheless could also, and with no inconsistency, write that the Irish economist William Thompson of County Cork had, in 1826, 'expounded theories like those of Marx before Marx was out of swaddling clothes'.

In short, there was already a living tradition for Marx to inherit. This in no way detracts from the originality of his thought: it would be thoroughly unmarxist not to acknowledge that the development of his thought was at the same time a development of the thought of others. For his philosophy he had drawn upon Hegel and Feuerbach in particular, again taking what he needed from them, rejecting the rest. From this evolved Marxism, the socialist philosophy which bears his name. One may say that Marx became a fully fledged Marxist with publication of his *Economic and Philosophic Manuscripts* in 1844.

By the time he died in 1883 there were political parties right across Europe and elsewhere which to a greater or lesser extent accepted Marxism as their political creed. But by then many were already busy 'revising' it. Marx would have said that they were betraying it, robbing it of much of its revolutionary content as they adapted it to the parliamentary democracies of which they had become an essential part.

Marx's socialism was in its very essence revolutionary. He believed that the world could and should be changed. that the massive philosophical, economic and political system which he had fathered provided the means by which it could be done. For Marxism was a science, too, the science of change and change-making.

There had been a time when he had reason to hope that his socialism would be adopted by the whole working-class movement across the world, that the new socialist parties everywhere would accept and act upon his revolutionary teachings. This was when the International Working Men's Association—the First International—was founded in 1864. Briefly it came under his influence and leadership, accepted his ideas. But it was already torn apart by squabbles between anarchists, 'reformists' and his own followers long before he died.

Here and there one found small groups of his disciples earnestly trying to apply what they considered to be the pure Marxist doctrine to their own national situations. In England there was the doctrinaire Social Democratic Federation from which William Morris, artist, designer and socialist campaigner, broke away to form the Socialist League. This in time was captured by the anarchists. Everywhere the authentically revolutionary Marxists were in a minority. Their influence existed within the wider labour movement but the revolution for which Marx worked himself to death seemed further away than ever.

The capitalism he had laboured to overthrow was still expanding. Steadily if grudgingly the employing class was responding to trade union and other pressures to raise the standard of life of the working class. The workers' representatives in parliament and elsewhere tended to reflect the optimistic belief that perhaps after all they might have some sort of stake in the system. This 'establishment' approach was dominant in the (Second) Socialist International which was at its strongest when the 1914 war pitilessly shattered many such illusions and demonstrated that workers of opposing sides could still be persuaded to go out and kill each other in a 'capitalist' war despite their membership of socialist parties.

THE BOLSHEVIKS

It was Vladimir Ilyich Lenin (1870–1924), leader of the Russian Bolsheviks, who more than anyone restored to Marxism its revolutionary content. Lenin, it has been said, put teeth into Marxism. He erected on Marx's revolutionary philosophy an organisation, the Bolshevik Party, equipped with Marxist theory, totally devoted to, and organised for, the making of revolution. Its purpose would be to launch Russia on the road to Communism. This meant first overthrowing the existing political and economic system.

The Bolsheviks, under Lenin's leadership, successfully achieved the seizure of power in October 1917. After years of civil war they finally established Soviet power right across the old Tsarist empire. The Russian ruling class was overthrown, the economic and political basis of its power destroyed, a new-type State machine created. In place of the Tsarist autocracy there was established a 'dictatorship of the proletariat' headed by the Bolshevik Party. This was precisely what it said, a dictatorship. But, the Bolsheviks argued, this would be a dictatorship of the many over the few, whereas the one which had been demolished was a dictatorship of the few over the many.

The dictatorship was seen as but a transitional stage on the way to the greater freedom of socialism. Beyond that lay the unprecedented freedom of fully evolved Communist society.

The Bolsheviks did not, it must be emphasised, overthrow some enlightened, smooth-working, democratic regime, but a very harsh, inefficient, corrupt and decadent autocracy due on any reckoning to move off the stage of history. Liberals and lovers of freedom everywhere had for long deplored its flagrant injustices. Its downfall at the hands of the revolutionary masses was therefore welcomed by people who had never heard of Lenin and knew little or nothing of Marxism. Many of the working people of Europe had been engaged in bitter class battles right up to the eve of the 1914 war. To these the ending of the Russian despotism was at one and the same time a cause for rejoicing and a challenge to rise up and throw off their backs their own exploiting classes. The collapse of the Tsarist regime (which had been described by Lenin as 'a prison house of nations') had its repercussions, too, among peoples just awakening to national consciousness but still living under colonial rule.

Marx taught that economic crises and wars were normal to the capitalist system and must sooner or later contribute to its undoing. When World War I came Lenin declared it to be an imperialist war in defence of profits, in which workers could have no interest except to the extent that they might turn it into a civil war. The idea was not entirely novel: Irish Republicans were at the same time popularising the idea that Britain's war was Ireland's opportunity.

Repeated, humiliating and costly Russian defeats on the Eastern front, along with the hardships endured by the civilian population as the economy neared total breakdown, provided the Bolsheviks with the opportunity they needed. The Tsarist regime fell, a weak government which lagged behind the militancy of the masses temporarily took over and

Lenin returned from Switzerland to complete the revolution.

Capitalism did indeed seem to be disappearing from the scene in the way Marx had foretold and according to the Marxist rule book. There were good Marxist reasons to suppose that the revolution would not be confined to Russia. This could become the classical 'general collapse of capitalism' with one revolution following fast on the heels of another.

Soon the German armies on the Western front also were meeting with defeat. There were mutinies, riots and abortive, semi-spontaneous risings. Inspired by the Russian example, Left-wing socialist and Marxist groups tried to turn the disaffection of the armed forces and the discontent of the masses to good account. Short-lived soviets—or workers' and soldiers' councils—sprang up. But there was no well organised Bolshevik-type party to provide the necessary leadership. Conditions were not yet ripe for successful revolution and the whole movement was effectively beheaded when the revolutionary socialist leaders Karl Liebknecht and Rosa Luxemburg were brutally murdered by Prussian army officers.

Under the Communist leadership of Bela Kun a Soviet regime was established in Hungary. It lasted twelve months before being crushed by the counter-revolution.

Troops of the victorious Allies, impatient for demobilisation and furious at being thrown into an ill-conceived war of intervention against Russia, staged mutinies. Twenty-six French war ships and troops of fourteen regiments in 1919 refused to go into action when told that they were to fight against the infant Soviet regime. To the mutiny of the Black Sea Fleet, in particular, was attributed the decision by the French Government to withdraw from the war of intervention. The mutiny was led by André Marty, later to become one of the top leaders of the Communist Party.

There was widespread discontent in both the British army and navy with numerous outbreaks of mutiny, whilst civilians of various shades of Left-wing opinion made a brief attempt to form workers' councils inspired by Russia's soviets. Ireland, which was on the eve of its own national liberation struggle, had already lost its one outstanding Marxist leader with the execution of James Connolly. Even so, the Red Flag was run up over some factories and creameries which had been taken over by the workers employed in them. Here and there other workers set up revolutionary councils to which they gave the name of soviets, although the evidence suggests that they had little knowledge of the situation in the newly established Soviet Union and still less of the ideology which its leaders professed.

The round of successful revolutions which Lenin, Trotsky and other Bolshevik leaders believed to be essential if their revolutionary regime was not only to survive but to become a genuinely socialist one failed to materialise. Hopes had been raised only to be dashed again. Russia must for the moment go it alone. Revolution had indeed been in the air. Men who had faced death in the trenches during the most senseless and brutal war of history had no desire to go back to the old injustices. But the conditions which had led to the wave of semi-spontaneous risings changed as governments re-established some form of stability and so did the mood. Workers became more preoccupied with the search for jobs or the threat of unemployment than with the long-term hope of a just society.

Out of that period, however, emerged Communist parties all over Europe, in North America, South America, a number of countries of Asia, South Africa, all modelling themselves on the Russian one by which they were encouraged and assisted. In most cases these new-type parties were a combination of various rival Marxist and Communist-anarchist groups and individuals coming together, directly inspired by the Bolshevik Revolution, in an attempt to sink their differences and become a serious revolutionary force.

By the time they had sorted out their differences—usually shedding a number of members on the way—and established their organisation, the objective conditions for revolution had passed. But fired with the thought of the coming struggle for power, they were the people who were least likely to notice this. Many of them, like early Christians awaiting the Second Coming, continued to think that the revolution was just around the corner long after any hope of it had disappeared. As late as 6 May 1926, during the British General Strike, Trotsky could write that the revolutionary change in Britain might possibly come at 'an early date'.[1]

In 1848 Marx and his collaborator Frederick Engels had ended their famous *Communist Manifesto* with the resounding slogan: 'Workers of the world unite, you have nothing to lose but your chains, you have a world to win!' Now it seemed that chains might indeed be shattered, not just in Russia, which had been one of the most 'soft' and inefficient sectors of the capitalist front, but right across the earth. Provided, that was, that the workers of the world could be united. This was necessary, not only to achieve their own emancipation, but also, it was agreed, to ensure the survival of the Soviet Union, the first workers' State, upon which incidentally the political future of the Communist parties themselves to a great extent depended.

Marxists generally had for long held, and Lenin and Trotsky now insisted, that the one great safeguard for the continuance of a revolutionary regime would be continuing revolution elsewhere. Without this, Russia would be unable to develop into a socialist society for it would be constantly under the threat of destruction by the combined imperialist forces from without, and by subversion by imperialist hired spies and saboteurs from within.

To any Communist it seemed obvious that a new Communist International should be created. The First International had been destroyed by dissension; the Second had sold its soul. But now in a world where a Communist base was already established, and in this period of wars and revolutions, a new one ought surely to be able to survive and to retain its revolutionary Marxism, come what might.

And so, under Lenin's inspiration and direction the Third International (the 'Comintern') was brought into existence. Marx's First International had been a loosely organised affair consisting of groups holding widely differing philosophies, views and beliefs. Lenin's Third International, reflecting his approach to the need for parties of a new type, of disciplined, professional revolutionaries, was one in which all were expected to keep in step organisationally and ideologically too.

Thus the inner-party discipline voluntarily accepted by members of the various Communist parties affiliated to it was imposed upon those parties themselves. This established a pattern of *de facto* Russian supremacy which was to cause trouble later on when it was carried over to relations with the new Communist ruled States which came into existence at the end of the World War II.

In his closing speech at the International's First Congress, on 6 March 1919, Lenin declared that 'the victory of the proletarian revolution all over the world is assured.' Here, in effect, was an international revolutionary army with its high command in the Soviet Union, its various units in the capitalist

strongholds and in the colonies as well. That, at any rate, was
how it was presented to the affiliated organisations at the
time. Under Stalin's rule it later became little more than an
instrument of Soviet foreign policy. But that was not how the
Communists themselves saw it.

Like Lenin, the infant Communist parties saw the Comintern
as an important means by which the revolution could, with
Russia's aid, be spread. What could not be foreseen at the
time of its founding, however, was that the Communist
Party of the Soviet Union would continue for a generation
to be the world's only ruling Communist Party; and that this
circumstance would lead to the International itself, and its
constituent parties, being dominated and dictatorially controlled by the C.P.S.U.

That statement, however, needs qualifying for warning
noises came from within the Marxist camp itself. In April
1919, Trotsky, for ever conscious of the need for the advance
to socialism to be a joint effort, not a solo performance, wrote
(in *Thoughts on the Progress of the Proletarian Revolution*) that
the Russian proletarian dictatorship would be able to con-
solidate itself finally and to develop a genuine, all-sided
socialist construction, 'only from the hour when the European
working class frees us from the economic yoke and especially
the military yoke of the European bourgeoisie, and having
overthrown the latter, comes to our assistance with its
organisation and its technology.'

He forecast that the leading revolutionary role would then
pass to the working class with the greatest economic and
organisational power. 'If today the centre of the Third International lies in Moscow then tomorrow—of this we are
profoundly convinced—this centre will shift westward: to
Berlin, to Paris, to London.' This was a frank admission that

backward Russia was not the ideal leader of the International. Yet, given the failure of the revolution to spread 'to Berlin, to Paris, to London,' and in view of Lenin's attachment to the authoritarian concept of 'centralised democracy'—which Trotsky had criticised when it was first formulated in 1902—all the international strings would automatically remain in Russian hands.

Russia's domination of the world Communist movement was to become a far greater issue of course when the U.S.S.R. ceased to be the only Communist-ruled State and other Communist parties such as the Yugoslav, Chinese, Hungarian and Czechoslovakian parties found themselves as rulers too.

Lenin suffered a stroke in March 1923 which left him almost totally incapacitated. Nonetheless on the eve of his death he managed to send to the Thirteenth Congress of the Communist Party of the Soviet Union a 'Letter to the Congress' which later came to be known as the Lenin Testament. In it he showed his deep concern at the jockeying for leading positions which had already started within the party, then gave his own assessment of various prominent members of the Central Committee.

Of Stalin he wrote: 'Comrade Stalin, having become General Secretary, has concentrated boundless authority in his hands, and I am not sure whether he will always be able to exercise that authority with sufficient discretion.' On his death bed, it seems, Lenin was beginning to appreciate where concentration of power at the top of the party and of the dictatorship of the proletariat could lead.

He suggested that they 'think over a way of removing Stalin' from his position and appoint somebody else, 'differing in all other respects from Comrade Stalin by one single advantage, namely that of being more tolerant, more loyal, more polite and considerate to the comrades, less capricious etc. This circumstance may appear to be a negligible trifle but it is not a trifle, or it is a trifle which can acquire decisive importance.'[2]

Stalin, however, at that moment was useful to other leaders who were resisting any possible growth in Trotsky's influence. Congress delegates were persuaded to support his continuing as General Secretary on condition that he heeded Lenin's criticisms and drew the necessary conclusions from them. As history shows all too clearly, Stalin did nothing of the sort. A bitter fight within the leadership, which was part power struggle, part conflict over policy, continued throughout the remainder of the 1920s until in the end every rival to Stalin, actual or potential, was either brought by him to heel, banished or physically liquidated. Execution at the decree of their own leader was, in fact, the fate of the majority of the men who made the revolution.

By the early nineteen-thirties Stalin had absolute control over the party and the lives of the people of the Soviet Union. In addition, he had put his stamp on what was now called Marxism-Leninism-Stalinism. He toughened up the dictatorship, taking more and more power into his own hands as time went on. This no doubt may be attributed to a pathological mania for power but it was also related to his single-minded determination to make the vast but as yet backward Soviet Union into a modern, highly industrialised technological society and at the same time the world's first socialist one.

Because the Communist movement throughout the world was linked with the Communist International which Russia dominated, this meant that to a great extent a whole generation of Communist Party leaders during the formative years of the movement's life were moulded by Stalin's thought. Consequently, the non-Stalinist Marxism one finds within the traditional Communist parties, and also that of the New Left, today, can only be understood in the light of Stalin's version of Marxism and the current reaction away from it. For as Jean-Paul Sartre put it:

> From the moment the U.S.S.R., encircled and alone, undertook its gigantic effort at industrialisation, Marxism found itself unable to bear the shock of these new struggles, the practical necessities and the mistakes which are always inseparable from them. . . . Now the Party leaders, bent on pushing the integration of the group to the limit, feared that the free process of truth, with all the discussions and all the conflicts which it involves, would break the unity of combat; they reserved for themselves the right to define the line and to interpret the event.[3]

One can only speculate whether it was, in fact, Marxism as such, or Marxism-Leninism-Stalinism that failed to 'bear the shock'. Remembering the straitjacket into which Stalin forced Marxism there can be little quarrel with Sartre when he goes on to declare that:

> For years the Marxist intellectual believed that he served his party by violating experience, by overlooking embarrassing details, by grossly simplifying the data, and above all, by conceptualising the event *before* having studied it. And I do not mean to speak only of Communists, but of all the others—fellow travellers, Trotskyites, and Trotsky sympathisers—for they have been *created* by their sympathy for the Communist Party or by their opposition to it.[4]

FURTHER READING
Chapter 1

Franz Borkenau, *European Communism*, London: Faber & Faber, 1953.

James Connolly, *Labour in Irish History*, Dublin: Irish Transport & General Workers' Union, 1934.

C. Desmond Greaves, *The Life and Times of James Connolly*, London: Lawrence & Wishart, 1961.

V. I. Lenin, *What is to be Done?*, Moscow: Foreign Languages Publishing House, (undated).

V. I. Lenin, *Selected Works*, *V*, London: Lawrence & Wishart, 1936.

John Lewis, *The Life and Teachings of Karl Marx*, London: Lawrence & Wishart, 1965.

Franz Mehring, *Karl Marx: The Story of his Life*, London: Allen & Unwin, 1936.

Andrew Rothstein, ed. and tr. *History of the Communist Party of the Soviet Union*, Moscow: Foreign Languages Publishing House, 1960.

Jean-Paul Sartre, *Search for a Method*, New York: Alfred A. Knopf, 1967.

Leon Trotsky, *Where is Britain Going?*, London: Communist Party of Great Britain, 1926.

2 Basic Aims and Beliefs

WHAT is Communism all about? What are today's Communists trying to do? What do they believe? With more than fifty years of experience of successes and failures, of organisational principles and fundamental beliefs put to the test of time and practice, different Communists would give different answers to those questions. Just as, for that matter might different Christians if asked similar questions about their Christianity.

But Marxism is still what above all else they have in common, even though this may be given different emphases and interpretations in different countries or even as between individual Communists. A somewhat revised version of Stalin's Marxism is still basically that of many organised Communists. There are those to whom any revision is just so much heresy; others who are trying to de-Stalinise large areas of their Marxist thought as thoroughly as possible,

feeling their way along to see just how far they can go within
the limits set by the party.

In 1960, with Stalin dead and to some extent dethroned, the
Soviet leaders felt that a new Marxist manual was required.
So they commissioned *Fundamentals of Marxism-Leninism*,[1] a
book which reflected both the hold which Stalinism had on
Communist thought and also the tug-of-war between the old
attitudes and the attempt to break from them which had been
started by Nikita Khrushchev. It is a struggle which continues
to this day.

Described by its publishers as 'the most complete and
authoritative account yet published of the theory and practice
of world Communism', it is nearly 900 pages long, the work
of a team of Russia's leading scholars under the general
direction of 'Old Bolshevik' O. Kuusinen. In so far as there
is still an 'authorised version' of Communism this is it.

It sets out to explain the basic propositions of Marxism-
Leninism and to describe its goal: Communist society. This
latter, it tells us in a grand flourish at the end of the book, is
'a matter of the not very distant future'. So let us start with
the goal:

'Communism is a society that puts an end to want and
poverty once and for all, assuring the well-being of all its
citizens. . . . It removes the barriers which hampered the
development of the productive forces, and makes it possible
in time to create the large material and technical basis essential
for the achievement of an abundance of the good things of
life. . . .'

Quoting Nikita Khruschev it tells us that 'Communism
will bring man not a lordly life in which laziness and idleness
prevail but a life of labour, an industrious, cultured and
interesting life!' 'Hence', it continues, 'whatever the develop-

ment of technology, whatever the victories of science, the slogan "from each according to his ability" will remain the immutable principle of the Communist system.'

It goes on: 'Communism introduces a mode of distribution of material and spiritual benefits which is based on the principle of "to each according to his needs". In other words, each man, irrespective of his position, of the quantity and quality of labour he can give society, receives from society gratis everything he needs.'

Under the heading, 'The Free Man in the Free Society' it asserts that 'Communism is the most just social system. It will fully realise the principles of equality and freedom, ensure the development of the human personality and turn society into a harmonious association, a commonwealth of men of labour.' And, again: 'The supreme goal of communism is to ensure *full freedom of development of the human personality,* [authors' italics] to create conditions for the boundless development of the individual, for the physical and spiritual perfection of man. It is in this that Marxism sees genuine freedom in the highest meaning of this word.'

It describes the changes which will occur and then says: 'All these changes are an inalienable part of the communist re-making of society, which will result in the disappearance of all traces of disunity and isolation in the relations between peoples.'

Paraphrasing and embroidering the writings of Marx and Engels and building up to the grand finale, the authors declare:

It is with the victory of communism that the real history of humanity in the loftiest meaning of this term begins. Man differs fundamentally from all living creatures in that his intellect and labour save him from having to passively adjust himself to his environment, enable him to remake this environment in conformity with the interests and needs of mankind. And although mankind has existed for many thousands of years, it is only communism that ushers in the era of its full maturity and ends the prolonged prehistory when the life of each man individually and the life of society as a whole were shaped by alien forces, natural and social, which were beyond man's control.

The victory of communism enables people not only to produce in abundance everything necessary for their life, but also to free society from all manifestations of inhumanity: wars, ruthless struggle within society and injustice, ignorance, crime and vice. Violence and self-interest, hypocrisy and egoism, perfidy and vainglory, will vanish for ever from the relations between people and between nations.

Seen in those terms, Communism is an ideal, a dream of the good society. It is not an ignoble dream. Even though it all sounds so very different from, say, Soviet society as we know it, the Communist, equipped with a knowledge of Marxism, believes that it can and will be achieved.

The passages I have quoted at some length—and there are many more equally quotable ones—were not intended as just so much Communist pie in the sky or dope for the masses. The authors were not just propagandists—although there is clearly a propaganda element in the presentation of their case —they were serious, scholarly men who wrote like this precisely because they were steeped in the thought of Marx, Engels, Lenin and, since they were shaped by the period in which they grew up, of Stalin too.

Karl Marx, the philosopher, economist, social scientist who

spent half his life in the British Museum poring over dusty government reports, diagnosing the ills of society, believed in that goal. So did his friend and collaborator Frederick Engels, industrialist and scientist. Lenin, too—and there never was a man who could cut more ruthlessly through the unrealities to get to the nub of an argument or to the hard facts of a situation.

SCIENTIFIC SOCIALISM

Their belief in the Communist goal rested firmly on their own Marxist approach to man and his world. It is shared by their followers today. In dialectical and historical materialism they believed they had the key to an understanding of why development occurs both in the physical universe and in human society. Paradoxically, it might seem, they believed in the reality of their ideal precisely because their socialism was not 'idealist', or utopian, but 'scientific'. Marxism was the science of change and change making. They wanted to change the world and here was the guide and the dynamic which would make it possible.

Marx claimed that his socialism was not based upon vague hopes for a better world, but upon an analysis of society, past and present, which enabled him to trace the main movements in history. Since these were subject to identifiable dialectical laws, those who understood the way those laws operated could also predict what would be the main pattern of development in the future. The processes at work in contemporary society, understood aright, could be used to ensure that the future would be socialist.

His studies led him to certain important conclusions, revolutionary in their content, and dynamically revolutionary in their application, about the nature of the world in which man lives and his role in it. These form the basis of what has come to be known as Dialectical Materialism and Historical Materialism. It is from these that all Communist policies, strategies, tactics flow if they are authentically Marxist. 'The philosophers', wrote Marx, 'have only interpreted the world in various ways; the point however is to change it.'[2] But the starting point must be a correct interpretation of the world.

Basic to Marxist belief is the idea that this is a purely material world and that man is therefore a purely material creature subject and responsive to the same laws. There is no God, no supernatural life, no human soul, no life after death. This makes Marx an atheist, but to be fair to him he was, unlike many of his followers, no crudely militant one. One may doubt whether he would have approved of Moscow's notorious and outdated anti-God museum, and he would probably have had little patience with the antics of the League of Militant Atheists, sponsored internationally by the Communists of the twenties and thirties. Marx was far more interested in discovering and striking at the causes of injustice, exploitation and human misery in which he believed religion had its roots, than at religion as such, even though he was not above tilting at it.

Religion, he wrote in a famous passage, is 'the opium of the people'. In appropriate circumstances an opiate is, of course, not necessarily a bad thing. The most humane thing one can do for a man writhing in agony may be to give him a drug. And so, if one is to understand the point that Marx was making one needs to put the quotation in its context:

> *Religious* suffering is at the same time an *expression* of real suffering and a *protest* against real suffering. Religion is the sigh of the oppressed creature, the sentiment of a heartless world, and the soul of soulless conditions. It is the *opium* of the people.

The abolition of religion as the *illusory* happiness of men, is a demand for their *real* happiness. The call to abandon their illusions about their condition is *a call to abandon a condition which requires illusions.* The criticism of religion is, therefore, *the embryonic criticism of this vale of tears.* . . .[3]

Marx reasoned that man throughout the ages has in important respects been the plaything of physical and, increasingly as his society has developed, of man-made forces which determine his fate, yet over which he has little control. Give him an understanding of the processes at work in the world and in society and he will be equipped to change both so that in time he will become the master of his own destiny. God would be redundant.

DIALECTICAL MATERIALISM

Man, even though a relatively highly developed creature, is subject to the laws that govern the rest of matter. What goes up, as we all know, has to come down. But there are other, dialectical, laws which Marx and Engels held were operative at all times and in all places. Modern Marxists, including some Western Communist party philosophers, now question the universality of these laws. This would have been unheard of in the past. It is still a cause of dispute and, among some of the older Communists, disapproval. In the British Communist Party such views, even though contested, are permitted; in some other Western parties to publicise them can still lead to expulsion. However, let us look at the 'orthodox' teaching first.

Matter, Marxists are agreed, is forever in a state of flux and change. Within it a process of development is constantly at work. In his book *Dialectics of Nature*, Engels put it like this:

> . . . the whole of nature, from the smallest element to the greatest, from grains of sand to suns, from protista to men, has its existence in eternal coming into being and passing away, in ceaseless flux, in unresting motion and change . . .[4]

How and why does the change occur? Find the answer to that and you have the key to accelerating and even directing the process so that man need no longer be manipulated by forces beyond his control. Drawing upon the teachings of Hegel, Marx discerned a pattern in the process of change which was of far more than philosophical interest. Of this Stalin wrote:

> Marxist philosophical materialism holds that the world and its laws are fully knowable, that our knowledge of the laws of nature, tested by experiment and practice, is authentic knowledge having the validity of objective truth . . .[5]

Neatly systematising the process (too neatly some Marxists would now say) Engels spelt out the laws of change as:

1. The transformation of quantitative into qualitative change;
2. The interpenetration and unity of opposites;
3. The negation of the negation.

Lenin arranged them in different order but it is the overall pattern, not the order, that is important. There are periods of gradual, quantitative, evolutionary change, often insignificant and imperceptible. These, as part of the process of development, pass to open, fundamental changes, qualitative changes or, if you like, revolutionary changes. From being gradual, development becomes rapid, there is abrupt change from one state to another. This revolutionary 'leap' occurs as the natural result of an accumulation of quantitative changes.

In the course of development what is new and emergent in due course cancels ('negates') what is old, only to become in time itself old and ultimately negated. The dialectical process, the struggle of opposites, is unending but not overall destructive, for it provides the impetus for change and development, the dynamic of history. Stalin put it like this:

> . . . dialectics holds that internal contradictions are inherent in all things and phenomena of nature, for they all have their negative and positive sides, a past and a future, something dying away and something developing; and that the struggle between these opposites, the struggle between the old and the new, between that which is dying away and that which is being born, between that which is disappearing and that which is developing, constitutes the internal content of the process of development, the internal content of the transformation of quantitative changes into qualitative changes.[6]

This world of constant movement and change, of renewal and development, can only be understood if it is seen as an integral whole in which things, phenomena, are organically connected with, dependent on and determined by, each other. Others may see phenomena isolated from surrounding phenomena, events isolated from other events but the Marxist will be conscious of their interconnection and look always for 'the cause behind the cause'.

HISTORICAL MATERIALISM

Apply this dialectical method to history and human society and its significance for revolutionaries becomes apparent. Accept the proposition that these same dialectical laws are at work in society and one accepts also that revolution is as normal to social change and as inevitable a part of it as is evolution.

Man became distinctively human, Marxists contend, when he first fashioned a tool with the conscious purpose of shaping matter to his will and advantage. What distinguished primitive man from the ape was work, his labour, use of tools applied to dead matter, or weapons used in hunting. Thus the instruments or 'means' of production were of fundamental importance, for they enabled man to master matter which hitherto had been his master. The means of production continue to be of prime importance for they determine man's power to produce and also the extent and level of his development.

Of vital importance, too, is who owns them. Prehistoric men having only the most primitive tools and weapons were obliged to live from day to day collectively, in groups, with only a minimum of food and the crudest of shelter to meet their day-to-day needs. They had little that was surplus to their immediate requirements. In effect theirs was of necessity a primitive, tribal Communist society, survivals of which one may still find here and there to this day.

However, once they had shaped simple implements and applied their labour to these in the cultivation of crops, a qualitative change occurred in their mode of life. They could now have a more settled existence and moreover they could from time to time produce food which was surplus to their immediate needs. With the creation of that surplus, expropriation and exploitation became possible. The expropriation, that is, of goods produced by the labour of others, and so the exploitation of that labour; with the stronger members of the group gaining domination over the weaker. Thus did separate, antagonistic classes emerge and with them that class struggle which has since been a feature of man's history.

The nature of each society, the class conflict, the form that exploitation has taken at any given moment in time have all been determined by the stage reached in the development of the means of production and who owns them. Here we have the conflict of opposites, the dialectical struggle, in the form of class war. As Marx and Engels put it in the second paragraph of the *Communist Manifesto* of 1848:

Free man and slave, patrician and plebian, lord and serf, guild-master and journeyman, in a word, oppressor and oppressed, stood in constant opposition to one another, carried on an uninterrupted, now hidden, now open fight, a fight that each time ended, either in a revolutionary reconstitution of society at large, or in the common ruin of the contending classes.

Within each succeeding society was the class which might in time destroy the existing ruling class, replace it, and introduce a new society. Its role would be progressive at first but the day would come when it, too, was ready to move off the stage of history with a new ruling class taking over. Or, as Marx and Engels warned, the two might go down to their common ruin. This latter point is of great importance since it qualifies the claim sometimes made by Marxists that the victory of Communism is inevitable. Lenin in particular stressed that whilst the existing society must some day, like all other things, come to an end, whether the revolution will triumph or the 'contending classes' go down to their common ruin will depend upon many objective factors. Not least, upon the existence of a revolutionary party equipped with Marxism to guide it.

Western feudal society provided Marx with a near-perfect case study as he sought to trace the dialectical process at work in man's history. The way in which today's capitalist class grew within feudalism only in time to overthrow it and itself become the ruling class is most frequently and understandably quoted by Communists as the way it works.

Runaway serfs who congregated for protection around the feudal castles and strongholds crystallised in time into urban populations, forming a new class of townsmen, neither feudal lords and landowners nor serfs. Here was the embryonic capitalist class. From trading with one another the people of the growing townships went on to seek trade further afield, spurred on by the profit motive. With improved navigation they were able to bring back to Europe the wealth of the Indies, the silks of China, the silver of Peru, creating 'wants' and 'musts', particularly among the prosperous members of this new middle class, the 'bourgeoisie'. As their productive capacity grew, along with the capital they were able to accumulate, so also did the need for constantly expanding markets, and the urge for increased political power too. A point was reached where the further development of this merchant capitalist class was restricted and frustrated by the feudal structures, now outdated, and the feudal lords who struggled to maintain them.

The feudal lords found it increasingly difficult to maintain their dominance once gunpowder had been invented. They could now no longer provide the protection to the townspeople which had once been their responsibility and they themselves were vulnerable to attack as never before.

Like the chick which, if it is to survive, must break the shell that once protected but now imprisons it, the emergent class was forced by the law of development into conflict with the old ruling class which ended in the overthrow of feudalism and the establishing of a capitalist system. True to form, the capitalist class began as a socially progressive force. But, like the one before it, it contained within itself the seeds of its own destruction, a class which would destroy it.

This was the proletariat, defined by Marx as 'the class of wage labourers who having no means of production of their own, are reduced to selling their labour power to live'.

The product of capitalism, the proletariat would inevitably be brought into irreconcilable conflict with the bourgeoisie, 'the class of modern capitalists, owners of the means of production and employers of wage labour'. What distinguishes this class is that it lives by the ownership of the means of production and the exploitation, for profit, of the labour of others; the basis of its wealth is unearned income derived from rent, profit or interest.

Accumulation of capital during its feudal, merchant-trader period, enabled this class to exploit to the full those inventions which launched the world into the industrial revolution and set it on the course to the modern technological society. For the new means of production included great factories filled with increasingly costly machinery. These enabled the industrial capitalists to exploit labour on a scale never before dreamed of. And this in turn enabled them to accumulate more capital, employ more workers, gain more profit, and so it goes on . . .

Marx spent half a lifetime studying the 'contradictions' of capitalism for it is these which must bring its downfall. Based on production for profit, capitalism tends always towards over-production. This leads to periodic economic crises. Pushed on by the search for profits the capitalists seek new markets overseas which brings them into conflict with those of competing countries as a consequence. This leads to ever recurring wars, fought in the name of justice, freedom or some such catch-call but which are in reality to safeguard the interests of the ruling class.

Put very briefly, Marxists have believed that these crises and wars would ultimately weaken capitalism to the point where the ruling class of one country after another would be unable any longer to govern and the mass of the people would be united in their hostility to that class.

Thus would come the collapse of capitalism, the proletarian revolution and, given correct leadership, the emergence of the new, socialist society. With this, in turn, would come the end of the class struggle and so, in due time, on to Communism, the classless society.

But why, assuming that capitalism does not come to an end with the contending classes going down to their common ruin, does it have to be socialism that so inevitably follows capitalism? Why not some other system? What makes the Communists so certain? Again we must go to the dialectical laws to find the answers.

One of the most profound contradictions of all within the capitalist system lies in the fact that although ownership of the means of production is private—a carry-over from the system which preceded it—production is social. That is to say, large numbers of people work together in the productive processes but the means of production still remain in private ownership. The larger the factory, the larger the number of men engaged under its roof to produce wealth for others, and the less hope is there of their ever themselves having a stake in the ownership.

Here is an in-built conflict, or contradiction. The contradiction is resolved only when the proletariat take the means of production out of private ownership and build for themselves a society based on social ownership. Only so will the workers themselves see that justice is done. Socialism is therefore the natural political philosophy for the proletariat.

It is not, however, just a question of social justice being achieved but also of the more politically conscious workers associating themselves with the operation of the dialectical laws under the leadership of men who, understanding the process, make themselves its willing instruments.

Then, in the words of the *Communist Manifesto:* 'The knell of private property sounds. The expropriators are expropriated.' Or, if you like, the transformation of quantitative into qualitative change, the revolutionary leap, has been achieved—with man's co-operation.

The foregoing is the admittedly over-simplified dialectical and historical materialism which was taught within the Communist Party and presented to the world in general for many years. It is pretty much what is still accepted by the rank and file Communists who were moulded by the Stalin period or who have been taught by those who were.

Marx's was an all-inclusive system. After him Lenin set about trying to systematise Marx's thought. Then Stalin in due course proceeded to fit Lenin's into a pattern even more rigid than that used by moral theologians of the past—and by some of the present day. 'Here are the problems: one, two, three, four. And here are the answers to them: one, two, three, four.'

In practice this means that Stalin was attempting to fit the entire universe, the whole of life, the destiny of the human race, into his own 'Marxist-Leninist-Stalinist' mould and to hand down the answers to its problems from on high. All this could be and was represented as a legitimate development of Marxism, a system which, if it has any meaning at all, should by its very nature be for ever open-ended and the very opposite of rigid. In fact, what was happening throughout the Stalinist period was that instead of Marxism itself developing and expanding it was contracting, shrivelling, becoming ever more closed and rigid.

The current trend among protesters of the younger generation to accept some form of Marxism whilst rejecting that of the Communist Party is in part a reaction away from that rigidity. And many of the intellectuals within the parties of the West are consciously attempting to escape from the Stalin straitjacket. It can be argued that this should make the Party more acceptable to the masses, but the facts point in the opposite direction. Revolutionary parties need not only revolutionary theories but also revolutionary situations—at least somewhere on the far horizon—in order to remain genuinely mass parties over the years. The alternative is to attempt to keep the mass membership but at the price of becoming virtually part of the Establishment.

FURTHER READING
Chapter 2

Maurice Cornforth, *Materialism and the Dialectical Method*, New York: International Publishers, 1960.

Frederick Engels, *Anti-Dühring*, London: Martin Lawrence, 1937.

Frederick Engels, *Dialectics of Nature*, London: Lawrence & Wishart, 1940.

Roger Garaudy, *Karl Marx: The Evolution of his Thought*, London: Lawrence & Wishart, 1967.

G. Glezerman and G. Kursanov, ed., *Historical Materialism: Basic Problems*, Moscow: Progress Publishers, 1968.

Antonio Gramski, *Prison Notebooks,* London: Lawrence and Wishart, 1971.

G. Kursanov, ed., *Fundamentals of Dialectical Materialism*, Moscow: Progress Publishers, 1967.

V. I. Lenin, *The Teachings of Karl Marx*, London: Martin Lawrence, 1933.

Franz Marek, *Philosophy of World Revolution*, London: Lawrence & Wishart, 1969.

Karl Marx and Frederick Engels, *The Communist Manifesto*.

George V. Plekhanov, *Fundamental Problems of Marxism*, New York: International Publishers, 1969.

Robert C. Tucker, *The Marxian Revolutionary Idea*, London: Allen & Unwin, 1970.

Gustav A. Wetter, *Dialectical Materialism*, London: Heinemann, 1958.

Gustav A. Wetter, *Soviet Ideology Today*, London: Heinemann, 1966.

4

3   The Party in Action

THE first modern Communist Party on which all others were subsequently modelled was hewn by Lenin early in this century from the Russian Social Democratic Party which, like similar parties of its period, was organised along broadly democratic lines. In the conditions then existing in Russia, however, it had necessarily to be an illegal organisation.

In a tradition firmly established by Marx himself, Lenin accepted that a Marxist party should have a programme of 'immediate' demands which corresponded to the most urgent needs of the working class. A longer-term aim should be the seizure of power as a necessary prelude to launching one's country on the way to Communism. It must, therefore, be a revolutionary party. As such it must not get bogged down in the fight for reforms as, for example, the 'revisionist' Marxists of Germany had tended to do. Once this happened there was little to distinguish such parties from non-Marxist idealist socialists of the type who dominated the British socialist movement.

To make a revolution, Lenin argued, one needs a revolutionary organisation. A party of the old type spent two-thirds of its time in long-winded discussion and was clearly not geared to making a revolution. There could be no revolutionary movement without a revolutionary theory. So a genuinely Marxist party must be firmly based on a knowledge of scientific socialism. Something more, however, was required than an organisation of armchair philosophers learned in Marxist theory but unable or unwilling to put it into practice. There were too many of these around already. The Russian Social Democratic Party had suffered from having a surfeit of 'pure' theoreticians and of 'pure' activists too. Needed were men who combined theory and practice.

For this a party of a new type was needed with a different form of organisation and an entirely different concept of what constitutes a political party. In the course of inner party struggle and fierce polemics with some of the other leaders Lenin thrashed out his ideas of what it should be like. These he embodied in his book *One Step Forward Two Steps Back: The Crisis in Our Party*, published in 1904.

Making a revolution was a serious business. The new model party must, he insisted, consist of 'professional revolutionaries'. These would be men totally dedicated to achieving the revolutionary purpose for which the party existed, willing to sacrifice and submerge themselves as individuals for it. When he wrote of 'professionals' he meant people who were not amateurs simply giving their spare time and thought to the party. The whole man, the whole of his life must be dedicated to the revolutionary cause.

PARTY ORGANISATION

A revolutionary Marxist party must be flexible, able to change
with an ever-changing situation—a good Marxist, 'dialectical'
concept, this. It must be ready, perhaps, to work above
ground one day and go underground the next; able to make
the fullest possible use of legality but able also to turn illegal
conditions to equally good account.

In this ever-changing world, it is natural and normal for
situations to be fluid and fast-changing. So, if the party was
to be fully effective it would need to be at once both flexible
and highly disciplined. It should be responsive to leads from
above. What was really needed was a type of organisation
which was to all intents and purposes a revolutionary army.
Members should have 'the mentality of the soldier of the
proletarian army'.[1] There should be unity of belief and unity
in action.

To achieve the desired results, power should reside at the
centre of the party. It is here, in particular, that the organisation
of that first Communist Party and all those which subsequently
modelled themselves upon it differed profoundly from
traditional, democratic parties. The most significant distin-
guishing characteristic was the centralised nature of its chain
of command.

This form of organisation, which came to be known as
'centralised democracy' or 'democratic centralism' is best
represented by a pyramid. At its apex is a small group of
full-time party functionaries, the political bureau. Then comes
the central committee (or executive), elected by a national
party congress, with disciplinary power over the lower organisations of the party. In practice the central committee came,
not to be elected on the basis of votes for various competing
individuals, but as a group or 'panel' nominated and endorsed

by the political bureau. The entire panel was either accepted or rejected. In the latter case new nominations were recommended by the 'Politbureau'. Beneath the Central Committee come District, Regional or Provincial committees, each responsible for its own geographical area, then Branch Committees based upon places of work or residence. At the bottom is the basic unit of the party, the group or cell.

Between congresses day-to-day decisions and policies are determined by the political bureau which seeks retrospective endorsement from the Central Committee.

In short, the political bureau, as Lenin conceived the party, was the high command of the revolutionary army, responsible for strategy and tactics and for imposing revolutionary discipline. Decisions were handed down from above, from one level to the next. At each the very full discussion took the form of how best the decisions might be applied to that particular area of activity. There might be differences of opinion but once the party 'line' was accepted every member was expected to operate it. The forming of factions, or opposition groups, within the party, would not be tolerated. 'Official Oppositions' might be all right for parties which made work within the parliamentary system the beginning and end of their activities, but there was no place for such luxuries in a revolutionary party.

This form of organisation is fairly typical of what one would expect to find in any illegal revolutionary body, but it is not normally that of a political party working in conditions of legality within the democratic system.

Lenin's insistence that this was what was required for a Marxist party became a matter of fierce controversy within the Social Democratic Party and contributed to the split which led opposing groups to go their separate ways as Mensheviks and Bolsheviks.

Similarly it divided the Left wing of many an established socialist movement when Communist parties began to spring up under the inspiration of the Russian Revolution. For example, Tom Bell, a foundation member of the British Communist Party wrote:

> Much difficulty was experienced in trying to educate the comrades to recognise the necessity for central direction and executive responsibility for political leadership: that it was not enough for executive members to come to the Central Committee, hear reports, ask questions and delegate their authority to one or two officials, leaving them the responsibility for carrying through the policy. Much discussion and educational work had to be carried on to get these comrades to realise their responsibilities as executive members, and to break them from the old social democratic theory of formal representation by districts. In short, it was a struggle for the recognition of democratic centralism in the party.[2]

The party was attempting to 're-educate' its members to accept a concept of organisation alien to that of the existing democratic tradition.

The British party, in common with many others, grew out of a number of existing Marxist and other splinter groups in and around the official labour and socialist movement. They were drawn together by a common desire to follow Russia's revolutionary example. Some of their leaders were rebels because they were individualists. These found it quite impossible to accept the unfamiliar, rigid discipline which meant an invasion of their own individuality but which the new Bolshevik-type party demanded of them.

A case in point was that of Sylvia Pankhurst, the leader of

the Workers Suffrage Federation and well-known suffragette. The Federation had opposed the war and had among its declared aims abolition of the capitalist system. Sylvia Pankhurst had her own paper, *Workers Dreadnought*, in which she was accustomed to express her own highly individual point of view. When she helped to found the Communist Party she brought with her not only her small organisation but also her paper which she regarded as her property. It was not long before she was resisting the Central Committee's demand that it be brought under the party's control with editorial policy dictated for her. In short, the party leaders, in accord with the demands of democratic centralism, believed it should be a party organ. When Sylvia Pankhurst refused to accept these directions she was expelled.

To unity of belief had to be added unity in action. So every paper and publication, every organisation for which the party was responsible or which it controlled, the entire party membership themselves, must come under unified and centralised direction and control.

It is rare for any two Irish politicians ever to be in total agreement for long. It is almost certainly the case that the discipline upon which the Communist Party insisted helped to lessen its appeal in Ireland. It helps also to explain the high rate of defections over the years.

Indeed, the first few years in the life of most of the Communist parties were marked by expulsions and defections until gradually the 'social democratically minded' and the 'romanticists' and 'adventurists' who wanted the revolution without having to accept the revolutionary discipline were sloughed off, leaving the field to those who accepted Lenin's new party concept.

With Stalin's accession to power the discipline was, if

anything, tightened so that the 'iron discipline of the Communist Party' came to be one of the features for which it was most noted.

THE PARTY AND THE UNIONS

From the first, Lenin believed that the party must work in and through other organisations. It must be prepared to engage in any form of activity which would further the revolutionary cause, particularly inside the working-class movement. Whilst doing so it must never lose sight of its goal, nor forget what all the activity was about. Short-term programmes were necessary but for the Marxist revolutionary, Lenin insisted, reforms could be of interest only in so far as they could be made stepping stones to revolution.

Trade unions and co-operatives were, for the serious Communist, so many potential 'transmission belts' to Communism. Party members who were trade unionists should aim to get acceptance for its policies and aim to convert their fellow unionists to a Marxist ideology.

This approach to the mass organisations was spelt out in the *Programme of the Communist International*. The party, it said,

> must secure predominant influence in the broad mass proletarian organisations (Soviets, trade unions, factory councils, co-operative societies, sport organisations, cultural organisations, etc.). It is particularly important for this purpose of winning over the majority of the proletariat, to capture the *trade unions*, [C.I.'s italics] which are genuine mass working-class organisations closely bound up with the every-day struggles of the working class.

To work in reactionary trade unions and skilfully to

capture them, to win the confidence of the broad masses of the industrially organised workers, to relieve and remove from their posts the reformist leaders, represent important tasks in the preparatory period.[3]

Said the Programme: 'The party must neither stand aloof from the daily needs and struggles of the working class nor confine its activities exclusively to them. The task of the party is to utilise these minor everyday needs as a *starting point* from which to lead the working class to the revolutionary struggle for power.'[4] [C.I.'s italics.]

Stalin made clear the different attitude of the Communist to that of the reformist who seeks only to improve the situation within the system, when he wrote:

> The revolutionary will accept a reform in order to use it as a means wherewith to link legal work with illegal work, in order to use it as a screen behind which his illegal activities for the revolutionary preparation of the masses for the overthrow of the bourgeoisie may be intensified. This is what the revolutionary utilisation of reforms and agreements in an imperialist environment means.[5]

Communists working in the 'reformist' trade unions took these things seriously. Using the unions as 'transmission belts for Communism', 'screens' behind which the Communist carried on his own work for his own quite different goals, was exciting and, more important, made very good sense from the Communist point of view. It frequently worked well as a technique, too, in so far as capturing the unions and bringing them under Communist control was concerned.

The technique, however, became much more difficult to operate and far less rewarding as others got round to reading their Lenin and Stalin or, seeing the technique in practice, came gradually to understand what was happening. It depends, of course, for its success on the ignorance or apathy of the non-Communist members of the organisations in which it is used. As a consequence it might by now be described as one of the Communists' wasting assets.

RUSSIA'S ROLE

Communist intentions became more suspect, too, and their activities correspondingly more difficult as others read the Leninist classics and from them learned what was supposed to be Russia's role in promoting revolution in the non-Communist world. Consider this for example:

> During this period the tasks of the Party in the domain of *foreign policy* are determined by the position of our Party as a party of international revolution. These tasks are:
>
> 1. to utilise each and every contradiction and conflict among the surrounding capitalist groups and governments for the purpose of disintegrating imperialism;
>
> 2. to spare no pains or means to render assistance to the proletarian revolution in the West;
>
> 3. to take all necessary measures to strengthen the national-liberation movement in the East;
>
> 4. to strengthen the Red Army.[6]

For struggling little Communist parties in such bastions of world imperialism as Britain and the U.S.A. it was heartening to have Stalin writing that the 'world significance of the October Revolution' lay not only in its constituting 'a great start made by one country in the work of breaking through the system of imperialism . . . but likewise in its constituting the first stage in the world revolution and a mighty base for its future development.'[7] It is not surprising that others found it a good deal less reassuring. The Communist Party image which emerged was one not easily shaken off.

Communists of the period were more aware of the advantages than the disadvantages in the situation. Unlike the workers of Russia, they would not have to rise alone. There was the increasingly powerful Soviet Union now on the world scene, allegedly ready to assist them when the day came.

Lenin had promised that 'the assistance rendered by the first socialist country to the workers and toiling masses of all other countries' would be expressed in the 'development, support and stirring up of the revolution in all countries.'[8] He even went on to talk of the victorious proletariat of the one socialist country rising against the rest of the capitalist world, saying that it would 'attract to itself the oppressed classes of other countries, raise revolts among them against the capitalists, and in the event of necessity, come out even with armed force against the exploiting classes and their states.'[9]

These largely unfulfilled promises of effective revolutionary aid disturbed what Jack London, the American author and early Marxist-socialist called 'the affrighted bourgeois mind', and certainly gave ammunition to the cold-war warriors of a later period. Even at the time they represented a hurdle which those attracted to Communism had to take—as did also the whole concept of party discipline, organisation and serious revolutionary activity. For those reared in a democratic tradition these things were hard to take.

To understand how it was possible for many rebellious workers and troubled intellectuals to nonetheless accept all this, along with the need to subjugate themselves as individuals to the party, one must see them in the context of their time.

THE COMMUNIST HOPE

On and off throughout the nineteen-twenties, thirties, forties and into the early fifties the Marxist–Leninist leaders and theoreticians were, under Stalin's guidance and tutelage, insisting that here was an eve-of-revolution situation. Admittedly there was an ebb and flow process at work, but this was in accord with Marxist thinking. The important thing was that the revolution seemed never far away.

Throughout the twenties the Communist International and its affiliates were insisting that the capitalist world was heading for a profound economic crisis and that another imperialist war was possible at any moment. This was, as the Communist International defined it, a period of ever recurring wars and crises—and Marxist hopes were based on a revolutionary situation emerging from either imperialist war or economic crisis. The revolution might thus come at any moment and good revolutionaries must see that they had oil in their lamps or, to get away from biblical metaphors to Marxist practicalities, they should be organised and ready to seize the moment of opportunity when it came.

The Great Depression came in the thirties. It took the form of Marx's crisis of over production and it looked as though it might be Lenin's moment of opportunity too. With horrifying speed, right across the capitalist world, machines, factories, whole industries ground to a halt. Men were thrown into the ranks of the unemployed, on to the human scrap heap—hundreds, thousands, millions and then, literally, in scores of millions. One did not need to have read very much Marx to believe that capitalism was now decadent, done for, collapsing.

As the process continued over the years not only workers living either with the reality or the spectre of unemployment but intellectuals, too, came to believe that capitalism was a bankrupt system with nothing left to offer mankind. This was not too eccentric a thought; there was a good deal of evidence to support it. As a system capitalism had brought industrial advance but it had now ceased to be a progressive force and had become retrogressive. It was time for it to move off the stage of history before it brought another imperialist war as well.

The crisis came and went. When the wheels of industry began to turn again in the mid- and late-thirties, those who benefited from the recovery and who lacked Marxist theory or socialist commitment might begin to come to terms with capitalism again. But for the others who had been attracted to Communism during the depression years, even the new, relative prosperity did little to restore belief in capitalism since the new situation began with and was a consequence of vast re-armament programmes launched in anticipation of the possibility of World War II.

One did not have to be a wild-eyed revolutionary to believe that the Communists had something relevant to say in a period of outrageous irrelevancies. Almost alone the Comintern and the Communist Party had warned that the capitalist crisis, the rise of Hitler and the rearmament of Germany foreshadowed the coming of war. Whilst others were pretending that the danger did not exist or still went on whistling to keep their spirits up, even when that danger was manifestly inescapable, Communist parties were making their preparations for its coming.

'Without a revolutionary theory there can be no revolutionary movement' was repeated over and over again in Communist circles. To provide them with that theory Stalin commissioned, and in part himself wrote, *The Short History of the Communist Party of the Soviet Union* (*Bolsheviks*). This was 'history' written for a purpose. Outrageously slanted and selective, it told the story of the rise to power of the Bolshevik party and of the consolidation of the dictatorship of the proletariat under Stalin's leadership. This was history as Stalin wanted it, Marxist theory as he decreed that it should be. It is not surprising that Stalinism lingers on.

In the late nineteen-thirties, sales of the *Short History* exceeded even those of the Bible, the world's best seller. But whereas most often the Bible is left unread the *Short History* was read avidly by thousands of Communists throughout the capitalist world. It was read in the colonies too, where new Communist parties were springing up, and in areas where isolated Marxist groups were just beginning to coagulate into parties. In short, a whole generation of yesterday's Communists and many of today's as well were moulded by it to a greater or lesser extent.

It was a massive exercise. In every unit of the party, discussion groups were led by well briefed tutors who had themselves been taught both its contents and the technique of drawing out its every lesson. The classes went on continuously over the years with one new course starting as another ended.

During the worst years of the economic depression the Comintern issued the slogan 'Towards Soviet Power'. This reflected its belief that revolution might soon be possible throughout the West. In his report on the 13th Plenum of the Communist International (December 1933), Harry Pollitt, British Communist Party leader wrote: 'The chief slogan of the Communist International is Soviet power and we here in Britain must now raise this question of *power* in all our daily work.' Pollitt urged that the British party should now popularise the aim of a Soviet Britain 'working out absolutely concretely and popularly, in every sphere of our propaganda and agitation, what is the Soviet solution in Britain of the crisis.'[10]

The thesis quoted by Pollitt ends with these words:

> The Plenum of the E.C.C.I. obliges all sections of the Communist International to be on their guard at every turn of events, and to exert every effort without losing a moment for the revolutionary preparation of the proletariat for the impending decisive battles for power.

When war was clearly just around the corner expectations within the Communist Party rose. The war would be terrible but out of it might come the revolution.

The Party became the spokesman for anti-war elements of all sorts but it knew what it wanted to get from the war when it came. Once again, the prospect of revolution did not appear as absurd then as it may now do in retrospect.

Thus throughout all the years from the formation of the first Communist parties in the post-World War I period right down to the early years of World War II Communists could believe in the possibility of an early victory for their cause. There was a basis for their feeling and behaving like revolutionaries. In these circumstances acceptance of the Party's revolutionary iron discipline, democratic centralism, subordination of the individual to the party, the very evident lack of interest it showed in the problems of the individual living in capitalist society—all these became tolerable where otherwise they might have been intolerable.

Given its own view of the situation, the party's form of organisation and discipline made it exceptionally effective in the job it was trying to do. Lenin had said that it should be the vanguard of the working class. Stalin in his *Problems of*

Leninism and in the *Short History* hammered this home so
convincingly that party members felt themselves individually
and collectively to be the spearhead of a revolutionary movement which was going to sweep away a rotten old system and
prepare the way for something new and infinitely better.
Party training was aimed at producing an elite which would
make the great industrial working class its main instrument,
the peasants and the intellectuals its allies.

Members were thrown into the thick of the fight wherever
they went, leading in factories, trade unions, co-operatives,
cultural organisations, prepared psychologically and by
training for the job. The individual's highest aim was to be
'a man of steel', like Stalin; a 'steel hardened cadre' who, along
with his comrades, provided a Marxist backbone to a vast
body of people for whom capitalism had now little or nothing
to offer.

Communists could not of themselves produce the collapse
of capitalism without the necessary objective conditions being
present. But the collapse was nonetheless inevitable. Sooner
or later it must come and they could, by exploiting capitalism's
contradictions, accelerate its coming. This would be done by
the use of well-chosen campaigns, by the successful leadership
of great mass movements. If they were unable, or insufficiently
equipped, to exploit it when it came then, as Marx had
foretold in the *Communist Manifesto*, the contending classes
might go down to their common ruin. Thus a small group of
dedicated, well-instructed, superbly trained men would rescue
their fellows from that ruin, turning what would otherwise
be a catastrophe into a great revolutionary leap towards an
unprecedently better future.

Meanwhile, there was a powerfully entrenched capitalist foe
to contend with. A social system to be overthrown. This

could be achieved only if they fought for Communism as though they were fighting a war. This 'war psychology' was a feature of Western Communist parties so long as they believed that their own sectors of the capitalist front could be made to crumble in the near future. The Stalinists among them still think in those terms, the others less so. For Communists of the Third World it is still the norm.

Stalin's writings read almost like military manuals. They tell the Communist reader that he must learn to know when to advance, when to retreat, how to discover the weak points in the enemy front, how to infiltrate the camp of one's opponent, posing as a friend—then rounding on him and destroying him; how to make allies, how to use them, when to drop them and, if need be, when to destroy them as well.

FRONT ORGANISATIONS

To any political minority trying to make an impact upon the larger public, allies are, of course, of immense importance. Come the revolution they could almost certainly be of decisive importance to the Communists. Without allies the Bolsheviks could not have seized power, though there were not many allies left by the time power had been seized and in due course consolidated.

It was recognition of this need for allies which led the Communist International to launch one united front campaign after another throughout its life. For this is what the united front is all about; and the same goes for popular fronts, national fronts, national liberation fronts, worker and peasant alliances and all the other 'fronts' created by the Communists over the years. They had this in common: each one had a programme aimed at providing 'solutions' to immediate pressing problems as their short-term goal, and the strength-

5

ening of the Communist revolutionary movement as their long-term goal.

Stated briefly and baldly the essence of the tactic consists in discovering popular slogans linked with genuine grievances around which joint activity can be developed and then, in due course, using this to strengthen the Communist Party and to destroy its foes and rivals.

The first united front was launched in June 1921 at the Third Congress of the Communist International. A majority of the existing Communist parties of the time were no more than a couple of years old at the most but it was already apparent that they could not make a revolution single-handed. Growing unemployment and the problems associated with the conversion of war economies to those of peace provided more than enough agitational issues for the first call for a united front.

In the forty years that followed there were Communist-initiated front campaigns in support of almost every good cause and against every bad one. Peace, defence of democracy, freedom of the press, freedom of speech, defence of wages and working conditions; even, during the second half of World War II, in some countries, victory for war. There were united fronts against racial discrimination, colonialism, war. Often, if the Communists had not campaigned on these issues no one would have done so. And the issues were real.

Sometimes, precisely because the Communists took them up, liberals and democrats who might have campaigned on them stood aside. This became increasingly the case as anti-Communist propaganda and bitter experience between them led non-Communists to accept that association with the Communists for a good cause meant being used by them for a bad one—Communism.

Most successful of all was the great Popular Front movement of the nineteen-thirties which literally brought millions of non-Communists into association with the party for the first time in their lives. Not all were 'suckers', still less were they all political ignoramuses. Some had grave reservations about Communism because of the rumours they had heard of dreadful things being done in Stalin's Russia. These reservations were, however, less powerful than they might have been precisely because such obviously lying propaganda had so frequently been indulged in by militant anti-Communists. The tendency among 'the fair-minded' was to reject nine-tenths of the horror stories out of hand and to assume that more than half of the others were probably lies anyway.

Still more important in a situation which to many seemed to offer little hope for the future was the belief that the Soviet Union and the Communists had their faces turned towards a better life. Communism, as it was known at the time, could look clean and decent by comparison with the Nazism and fascism established in so many countries of the West. The individual Communist, so selfless in his devotion to his cause, could look immensely better, man for man, than the men who were making fortunes out of preparations for war.

So a popular front against the threat of fascism had an obvious appeal. The first, in France, was quickly able to attract to itself people from other political parties, trade unionists, intellectuals who felt a moral compulsion to go into action or, at the least, to raise their voices against the devil they knew because he was on their very doorstep.

When Georgi Dimitrov, secretary-general of the Comintern, speaking at the Seventh World Congress of the Comintern in 1934, issued a call for a world-wide front against war and fascism the response was staggering. The background to his call explains its success. The Nazis had seized power in Germany and were by now pitilessly crushing not only Communists but intellectuals, liberals, trade unionists and socialists as well. All were alike threatened, it seemed, by any threat of fascism. France was not alone in having a growing fascist movement. The same went for half a dozen other countries of the period. To a greater or lesser extent fascism existed in every country of the capitalist world.

The end of World War I was a mere sixteen years behind. Relatively young men could still remember the carnage, the cynical sacrificing by army generals of scores of thousands of men in a single battle. The 'civilised' world was still littered with its widows and orphans. Now the Communists were saying that unless men and nations united, World War II was at hand. All the evidence pointed to the truth of this and to a conspiracy of silence on the part of the rulers of the period.

The Spanish Civil War gave added point to all this. For here were local fascists actually making war on a democratically elected liberal government and then gaining the armed support of Hitler and Mussolini. To go to the aid of the Spanish Government was a call to heroism which came like a breath of fresh air after years which had been notably unheroic. The Communists were visibly the vanguard. They were leading the battle and providing more than their quota of martyrs. Many of those who joined the Communists in the fight felt that they were engaging in a battle with evil things. They were, as it were, taking the side of righteousness, redeeming their generation.

It is necessary to understand this background if one is to comprehend the success of the Communists' unity appeal. It is true that in terms of influence, prestige and recruitment of new members, the Communist Party was invariably the one which did best out of any alliance. Most often its gains were at the expense of socialist parties in particular. Even so, the socialists could tell themselves that without the popular front they might have been crushed out of existence altogether by a victorious fascism.

Much of the Communist success was due to the fact that the issues they raised were real and that they were the first to speak out—or spoke most loudly—when others maintained a guilty silence. Had democracy been more authentic, more courageous, more vigilant, had democrats been more deeply involved in its processes, then appeals for united fronts might have fallen on deaf ears.

That the Communists were the ones who got most out of it is partly explained by the fact that most often they alone knew where they were going, they had clear goals, well-tried techniques. Where others were disunited the Communists had, on the basis of resignations, expulsions and purges, achieved unity of mind and purpose. Their form of organisation might seem an alien one in a democracy but it had helped to create a situation where a majority of their members were men of deep convictions. Their discipline, flexibility and lack of scruple which, taking the long view have proved to be political liabilities to them, gave them an immediate advantage over the rest.

Others might have very vague, mixed reasons for going into action at that time. The Communists were in the Popular Front because it was a thing of their own creation, intended to serve their purposes, help them to achieve their revolutionary goal, whilst at the same time being linked with very real and urgent immediate problems. Without their discipline, theory and commitment, tiny Communist parties could not have manipulated great mass organisations as was the case over and over again.

This brief glance at the Communist tactic of the united front is of much more than mere historic significance. Much of the suspicion of Communism which lingers as a powerful force in the organised labour movement today dates from that period. It has its origins in the fear that they might be used again. It is very relevant, too, to an understanding of what is currently occurring in the Communist world. For, as we shall see later, willingness on the part of some Communist parties and many individual Communists to accept the old discipline has weakened as the expectation of an early revolution has receded over the far horizon. The old insistence on every member of the revolutionary army keeping in step has weakened too. The same demands are not made on members today. Consequently the party's ability to manipulate others in the old way has been correspondingly weakened.

Even after the dissolution of the Comintern, Communists continued to use the united front tactic. Instinctively they still looked to Russia for guidance. By that time World War II had come and Russia was under attack. Communists needed no telling what was required of them. There was a period of national fronts in the countries of the Western allies aimed at building up support for the war. In the occupied countries, and in some of those of the Axis powers, united resistance movements were organised embracing just about all those elements the Communists had ever dreamed of bringing together.

The last great international round of united fronts, against the threat of World War III, took the form of a great united peace campaign in the nineteen-fifties. By then the party's unity and discipline were already being modified in accord with the needs—and more particularly the mood—of the post-war era. Even had they wished to, it is doubtful if the

Communists could since then have used the tactic in the same old way—at any rate in the West and in the more developed countries generally.

Communists still call for unity today. As their numbers decline so their need for allies grows. Only where revolution is still an early possibility can they hope to maintain the old discipline, command the same unquestioning, undeviating loyalty that characterised them for so long. In those circumstances, and given a politically unsophisticated public, the united front may retain its former usefulness in helping to bring Communism into power.

Elsewhere, attempts at forging a broad, mass unity of the Left have on numerous occasions in the recent past ended in failure or near fiasco. A conference called in Chicago with this purpose in mind ended in blows and with the movement more deeply divided than before. Another, in London, served only to highlight differences and to emphasise the absence of any genuine basis or will for united action. There has to be an element of crisis, or some basis for a great call to heroism, it seems, to bring people together today, and the united movements which then spring up last only so long as the crisis itself endures.

IRISH NATIONAL LIBERATION FRONT

At the time when armed Republican action against British rule was building up in Northern Ireland with the support of Republicans in the South, one might have guessed that a broad united front stretching from I.R.A. activists to Communists would have emerged, brought into existence by the Communists. After all, armed struggle in the form of mainly urban guerilla warfare had become a reality on Irish soil.

The Communist Party, existing in both North and South,

would be keenly aware of the political value of the widest possible front, quite apart from the important supportive role that such a front might assume. But the odds were against the Party.

It was, as we have noted, small and weak. Over the years it had, like other traditional Communist parties, become less revolutionary as it sought—with little success—to become more 'respectable'. It was also divided, with Stalinists and non-Stalinists challenging each other in their claim to orthodoxy whilst others, like the Maoists, Trotskyists and International Socialists, to the Left of it, challenged its very right to call itself revolutionary at all.

The I.R.A. and Sinn Féin, its political wing, had both split soon after trouble first flared up in the North. Among the major causes of this split had been the appearance in the movement's leadership of several Marxists and the belief that these, after 'infiltrating' had exerted a 'Communistic' influence upon it and had swayed its policies away from reliance upon the use of 'physical force'.

Their presence in the leadership was deeply resented in particular by some of the strongly anti-Communist old guard who led the break-away in 1970 to form what became popularly known as the 'Provisional' I.R.A., Sinn Féin.

The Provisionals were deeply committed to ending the border by violence. Their political programme, whilst vaguely described as 'socialist' had echoes of the social theories of Hilaire Belloc and may perhaps better be described as Distributist. They were the more consciously 'religious', and Catholic, of the two groups. This led, somewhat unfairly, to their being dubbed 'clerical fascists' by their opponents in the 'Officials' who just as deeply resented being lumped together as 'Communists'.

Marxists of any significant calibre are few and far between in Ireland but some of the best—and you could count these on the fingers of your two hands—were left in possession of some of the leading positions in the Official Sinn Féin and I.R.A. Even so, hardly any two embraced the identical version of Marxism.

A National Liberation Front emerged which predictably included the Communist Party and the Official Sinn Féin. It also had the support of a handful of dissident local Labour parties. But this was very far even from the popular fronts of the nineteen-thirties and certainly compared poorly with most other existing national liberation fronts in lands where armed struggle has erupted.

The 'Official' I.R.A.'s policy, as distinct from that of the more aggressive and widely publicised 'Provisionals', was the limited one of 'defence and retaliation' whilst the Official Sinn Féin attempted to politicise the masses, holding that this was a prerequisite for any significant bid for power. Their long-term aim was a united, socialist Ireland, with both political and economic power taken from its present rulers and passed into the hands of a revolutionary people. In the circumstances of the armed struggle it was the 'bang bang' boys (as the Officials called them derisively) of the Provisional movement who most often tended, perhaps inevitably, to have both the initiative and the publicity too.

FURTHER READING
Chapter 3

J. Bowyer Bell, *The Secret Army: A History of the IRA 1916–1970*, London: Anthony Blond, 1970.

Tim Pat Coogan, *The I.R.A.*, London: Pall Mall Press, 1970.

John M. Cammett, *Antonio Gramsci and the Origins of Italian*

Communism, Stanford, California: Stanford University Press, 1969.

G. D. H. Cole, *The People's Front*, London: Gollancz, 1937.

Douglas Hyde, *United We Fall: The Tactic of the United Front*, London: Ampersand, 1964.

Walter Kendall, *The Revolutionary Movement in Britain 1900–21*, London: Weidenfeld & Nicolson, 1969.

James Klugmann, *History of the Communist Party of Great Britain*, vols. I and II (other volumes in course of publication), London: Lawrence & Wishart.

V. I. Lenin, *One Step Forward Two Steps Back*, London: Lawrence & Wishart, 1941.

V. I. Lenin, *What is to be Done?*, Moscow: Foreign Languages Publishing House, (undated).

John Lewis, *The Marxism of Marx*, London: Lawrence & Wishart, 1971.

L. J. Macfarlane, *The British Communist Party*, London: Macgibbon & Kee, 1966.

4 Leninism: Ethics and Morality

IN a speech given to the Third All-Russian Congress of the Young Communist League on 3 October 1920, Lenin declared:

> We deny all morality taken from superhuman or non-class conceptions. We say that this is a deception, a swindle, a befogging of the minds of the workers and peasants in the interests of the landlords and capitalists.
>
> We say that our morality is wholly subordinated to the interests of the class struggle of the proletariat. We deduce our morality from the facts and needs of the class struggle of the proletariat.[1]

This is perfectly sound Marxism in the sense that Marxists hold that everything is for ever in a state of flux and change, that nothing is permanent, nothing is absolute. Necessarily, therefore, this must apply to moral and ethical codes.

Marxist-Leninists argue that the bourgeoisie adapts its ethics and its interpretation of the Ten Commandments according to its class interests. In time of peace, for example, you may be hanged for killing a man—if capitalism is to work smoothly some sort of law and order must be maintained. If war is declared, however, you may just as probably be executed for refusing to kill a man when your army superior tells you to do so.

If capitalists are able to adjust the rules of the game to suit their own purposes, so too, it is argued, may Communists. When they do so they can be even less inhibited, first because they do not even pretend to accept moral and ethical codes of religious derivation and secondly because, whereas the capitalist is going against his professed, religious principles, the Communist is acting in accord with his Marxist ones.

This has frequently given Communists an advantage over others since for them no holds are barred. Experience, however, has shown—and some Marxists as we shall see later have been ready to learn from this experience—that to go against accepted principles may itself be detrimental to the cause.

This is true in two ways: 1) Such a policy reinforces the belief that Communists are devious and unscrupulous, that their propaganda is concerned only with serving the Communist cause regardless of where the truth may lie. This puts potential recruits and allies on their guard and generally makes the Communists' attempts to establish normal relations with others more difficult. 2) An understanding of Communist theory has spread to non-Communists. Consequently governments and their representatives are expected to be more than usually on their guard when they have dealings with Communist governments. For if Communist morality is subordinate to the interests of the cause, then, it is held, any agreement

Communists may sign is not worth the paper it is written on.

In his *Left Wing Communism an Infantile Disorder*, Lenin discusses how to play one capitalist politician off against another or even against himself. In this case it is 'the Churchills and the Lloyd Georges' on the one hand and 'the Hendersons and the Lloyd Georges' on the other. He goes on to stress that it is necessary 'to combine the strictest loyalty to the ideas of Communism with the ability to make all necessary practical compromises, to "tack", to make agreements, zig-zags, retreats and so on.'[2]

Politicians who are not Communists are quite capable of zig-zagging, 'tacking', playing off one opponent against another. But the Communist has the advantage that when he does this he is acting in accord with his Marxist principles, being a good Marxist-Leninist and applying his dialectical materialism to his political activities. Whether in the long term it is really an advantage is open to debate—and there are some Communists today who are willing to question it.

In the early days of the British Communist Party disagreement arose on what should be the Party's attitude to reformist labour leaders who, calling themselves socialists, misled their working-class followers into thinking that it was possible to take a parliamentary road to socialism. Should the party give qualified support to such men or should it denounce them as scoundrels? Where there were no Communist Party candidates in parliamentary elections, should it support these 'reformists', assist them to get into the House of Commons, or should it work against them?

Lenin's advice was sought. It was that the reformist socialists should be given support, assisted on their way to parliament, in the belief that they would then reveal their bankruptcy as socialists. In the process they would discredit themselves in the eyes of the masses thus preparing the way for acceptance of Communists as the only genuine socialist leaders. 'I want', said Lenin, 'to support Henderson with my vote in the same way as a rope supports one who is hanged.'[3] Unprincipled? Yes, for a non-Communist. But for a Communist such action was consistent with his beliefs.

Lenin's 'professional revolutionaries' should bend everything to the cause. But this did not mean that they should never compromise. He wrote of the bourgeoisie:

> It is possible to conquer this most powerful enemy only by exerting our efforts to the utmost and by *necessarily*, thoroughly, carefully, attentively and skilfully taking advantage of every 'fissure', however small, in the ranks of our enemies, of every antagonism of interests among the bourgeoisie of the various countries . . . by taking advantage of every possibility, however small, of gaining an ally among the masses, even though this ally be temporary, vacillating, unstable, unreliable and conditional. Those who do not understand this do not understand even a grain of Marxism and of scientific modern socialism . . .[4]

Capitalists and opportunist socialist leaders alike resort to any sort of trick to prevent Communists from making progress and so Communists for their part should reply in kind:

> It is necessary to be able to withstand all this, to agree to any and every sacrifice, and even—if need be—to resort to all sorts of devices, manoeuvres, and illegal methods, to evasion and subterfuge, in order to penetrate into the trade unions, to remain in them, and to carry on Communist work in them at all costs.[5]

Trade union leaders themselves took to reading Lenin's

works and it is hardly surprising in the circumstances that some of the things he wrote proved to be unhelpful to the Communist cause. His 'frankness' may not have been unconnected with the fact that throughout his early years most of his writings were for illegal publications directed to his own followers, and that subsequently he was writing from within the dictatorship of the proletariat which he had established.

It will be noted that he recommends evasions etc. 'if need be'. In other words, Marxist-Leninists are not enjoined to use such methods the whole of the time. This would clearly be self-defeating and might even lead to the Communists as well as their opponents being deceived. But they should not hesitate to do so when it serves the Communist cause.

In recalling these very typical, well-worn passages from Lenin's works one is not just raking over embers better left to die. The leaders of the Communist parties across the world were reared in, and moulded by, Lenin's thought. His is still a major influence in all the parties, the dominant one in most. There are some party members who today are beginning to question their Lenin. They are still in a minority; in all but a few countries they are disapproved of by the party leadership, and in the Communist world Lenin is certainly accepted by the overwhelming majority as above criticism.

These aspects of Leninist thought and practice are relevant, too, because they represent major stumbling blocks for many non-Communists who, in good faith, would like to engage in dialogue with Marxists. They hang like millstones round the necks of those Communists who are genuinely trying to reform their organisation and their creed. And they help to explain the growing popularity of anti-Stalinist, non-Leninist forms of Marxism, particularly among the students and young intellectuals of the West.

The quotation with which we began this chapter was taken from a collection of writings and speeches published by Lenin in the early thirties. A quarter of a century later the Foreign Languages Publishing House, Moscow, produced another collection on the same theme under the title, *On Socialist Ideology and Culture*. In it, Lenin's speech to the Third All-Russian Congress of the Russian Young Communist League is given at greater length and in a different version.

We can gain a fuller insight into the Leninist approach to morality and ethics if we see his oft-quoted dictum 'our morality is wholly subordinated to the interests of the class struggle of the proletariat' in a somewhat fuller context. Here is the passage from which it is taken:

But is there such a thing as communist ethics? Is there such a thing as communist morality? Of course, there is. It is often made to appear that we have no ethics of our own; and very often the bourgeoisie accuse us Communists of repudiating all ethics. This is a method of shuffling concepts, of throwing dust in the eyes of the workers and peasants.

In what sense do we repudiate ethics and morality?
In the sense in which it was preached by the bourgeoisie, who derived ethics from God's commandments. We, of course, say that we do not believe in God, and that we know perfectly well that the clergy, the landlords and the bourgeoisie spoke in the name of God in pursuit of their own interests as exploiters. Or instead of deriving ethics from the commandments of morality, from the commandments of God, they derived it from idealist or semi-idealist phrases, which always amounted to something very similar to God's commandments.

We repudiate all morality taken apart from human society and classes. We say that it is a deception, a fraud, a befogging of the minds of the workers and peasants in the interests of the landlords and capitalists.[6]

Lenin had noted in the Tsarist Russia of his day, just as had Marx in the early industrial capitalist period of his youth, that religion was frequently used in the interests of an exploiting class.

He was being no more than a good Marxist when he stressed that materialism is the cornerstone of the whole philosophy of Marxism and that Marxism 'is as relentlessly opposed to religion as was the materialism of the Encyclopaedists of the eighteenth century.'[7]

Nonetheless, following in the steps of Marx, he condemned those who strove to 'declare war on religion' by trying to introduce into the programmes of Marxist parties explicit avowals of atheism or the notion that religion would be prohibited in socialist society: 'We must be able to combat religion, and in order to do this we must explain from the materialistic point of view why faith and religion are prevalent among the masses. The fight against religion must not be limited nor reduced to abstract-ideological preaching. This struggle must be linked up with the concrete practical class movement; its aim must be to eliminate the social roots of religion.'[8]

There are Christians who, while asserting that religion is something much more than the product of an exploitive society, would nonetheless feel that if Marxists aim to end exploitation, 'striking at the social roots of religion', this is no bad thing. Religion itself might be purified in the process.

In theory, the Marxist-Leninist should be content to 'educate the masses' in dialectical materialism, simultaneously working to change the social order to a point where men no longer need religion as an opiate. In practice the State which Lenin helped to found and others like it have not been content to leave it at that. Active harassment of religious believers has so far been a feature of each in turn. A period of active, large-scale persecution of believers followed by a period of discrimination against them has been a common characteristic.

This may in part be explained by the fact that Communist parties have generally attracted to themselves anti-clericals and militant atheists who have been given a more or less free hand to pursue their activities in the name of Marxism. But there is more to it than that.

Once one accepts the idea that morality must be subordinated to the interests of Communism there is only one guide left to the behaviour of the party and of the individual. Does it serve the cause of Communism? If it does it is right. If it injures the cause it is wrong. Couple this very conscious rejection of religion with that of God's commandments and it becomes possible to justify the persecution of anyone currently held to be unhelpful to the cause. This may include the party's closest allies, even respected party leaders. It is up to the individual and, in the last resort, the individual Communist leader, to decide what is in accord with the party's interests—and with no permanently valid moral or ethical code to guide him.

It can be argued that many of the worst cruelties of the Stalin era, now repudiated by thoughtful Communists as monstrous perversions of Marxism, sprang from this. Stalin could, with the support of most of his colleagues in the leadership, 'liquidate the kulaks as a class' (Stalin's words). This meant the elimination of vast numbers of small, family farmers who clung to their bit of land as ferociously as would, say, a French peasant or west of Ireland hill farmer.

As a Marxist-Leninist, Stalin believed that the whole of the means of production should be socialised. In the case of land, this meant collectivisation. Education, persuasion, gentle coercion were all used to bring the kulaks to accept collectivism, but without success.

In the end Stalin argued that this minority stood in the way of the party's efforts to bring the blessings of the Communist society to the whole of the people of the Soviet Union. Therefore, as a last resort, they should be liquidated as a class. It was a matter of simple arithmetic: some four million people denying the full achievements of Communism to 160 million. Therefore the four million should be sacrificed. Stalin could tell himself that this was a justifiable example of subordinating morality to the interests of the proletarian class struggle.

If a majority of the Old Bolsheviks were, in Stalin's opinion, similarly obstacles to Communist progress, possibly even its enemies, then, ruthless though it might seem, there was little reason why they should not be physically liquidated. This would at least ensure the end of their activities once and for all.

Accept Lenin's dictum on morality, link this to his concept of the dictatorship of the proletariat, and it is not too difficult to argue a case for sending the Soviet tanks into Budapest and ruthlessly crushing the Hungarian People's Rising. Had the rising succeeded and an anti-Communist regime been established, as was quite possible, then, with the Iron Curtain breached, the whole of Communist Central and Eastern Europe might have been threatened. It might be impossible to justify the action on the basis of accepted moral codes but it would not be too difficult for the Soviet leaders themselves to interpret Lenin's teaching in such a way as to leave them with clear consciences.

The same would apply to the invasion of Czechoslovakia by the Warsaw Pact countries. If those responsible for that invasion were convinced that the interests of Communism were at stake then any sort of action could, and should, be taken in the circumstances.

Many Marxist-Leninists of the Western world, including committed party members, have found it impossible to justify these actions. In some cases they have openly declared them to be distortions and perversions of Communism. Whilst respecting their position and commending their courage in speaking out one is entitled to question which are the more faithful disciples of Lenin, men who gave the orders or those who protested against them. There is a certain ruthless Marxist logic about Lenin's thought and practice and he himself clearly took the view that the Marxist can engage in any action, no matter how harsh, ride roughshod over any individual, or group of individuals, provided that he is convinced that this is the way to aid the revolution.

One could quote a dozen precedents for Hungary 1956 and Czechoslovakia 1968. Some obvious ones are Lenin's advocacy and launching of Red terror against counter revolutionaries at the time of the Bolshevik seizure of power; the crushing, in February 1921, of the revolt of the sailors of Kronstadt who had been in the very vanguard of the revolution (Trotsky's order to the troops was to 'shoot the Kronstadt "rebels" down like partridges'[9]); and the hunting down of the Ukrainian anarchists whose guerrilla activities in the early days of the civil war had been of immense value to the Bolsheviks.

Lenin had no difficulty in justifying the use of terror: 'Our Red terror is a means of protecting the working class from the exploiters, a means of suppressing the resistance of the exploiters,'[10] he wrote. According to his own criteria this was right.

It is indisputable that others beside Marxist-Leninists have been guilty of ruthlessness and cruelty, not infrequently in the name of a cause, an ideology, a religion, even of Christ. It may be argued that, for example, members of the Spanish Inquisition took the same view as Lenin, that the end, or the cause, justifies the means. As a consequence they did equally cruel things and presumably with similarly clear consciences. But any objective student of Christianity and Christian history would be likely to arrive at the conclusion that the inquisitors were, at the best, tragically misguided and that what they did was patently inconsistent with both the letter and spirit of the gospels. Contrary to the teachings of Christ, it was an affront to the moral and ethical codes which Christianity upholds.

A problem for today's troubled Communist is that it would be nearly impossible to show that the cruelties which have hitherto been features of the various Communist regimes are clearly against Marxist-Leninist teachings. Indeed they would appear to be consistent with, or at least legitimate interpretations of, Lenin's thought and practice. The Stalinist wing, which exists in every Communist party and is still very powerful in the U.S.S.R., defends every word and action of Lenin's, and seeks to perpetuate Stalin's even more ruthless interpretation of Leninist thought and practice.

Within some of the Western Communist parties, including those of Italy, Austria and Britain, are prominent members who are trying to wrestle with this problem. For many of these the Soviet reaction to the Hungarian People's Rising was the catalyst. They knew all the Marxist arguments, far more quotations from Lenin than we have room for here, to justify what was done. Yet they were still left troubled. Marxist-Leninist principles and practice had come into sharp conflict with human values and the conventional, orthodox moral code derived from what Lenin referred to as 'God's commandments'.

Typical of the trend in many parties was the discussion on Marxism and morals which continued over a period of several years in the columns of *Marxism Today*, theoretical organ of the Communist Party of Great Britain. The following quotes will indicate the way in which Marxist thinkers are attempting to rescue their party from the consequences of a narrow interpretation of Lenin's dictum:

> We know and frankly acknowledge that Communists *have* sometimes indefensibly lied, broken promises, even tortured and killed people or in other ways caused or allowed people to be hurt or degraded . . .
>
> Critics of Marxism, however, suggest another explanation. Communists, they suggest, have done morally indefensible things because they have not seen them to be so because they have been blinded by an immoral or anti-moral theory, by Marxism. For Marxism in ethics, it is argued, amounts to a form of moral relativism which asserts that moral principles are nothing but disguises for class interests and implies that they have no objective, general validity . . .
>
> It seems to me, therefore, that when we Communists are accused of violating some moral principle—e.g. that lying is wrong—we should not be satisfied, as too often we are, simply with joining in the relativist chorus of 'We don't believe in eternal moral principles': we don't, but we do or should believe that moral principles have validity if not eternally yet often within very wide limits. . . . [Martin Milligan, January 1965.]

What we are primarily concerned with in dealing with honest criticism of Marxist ethics (or at least of Communist morality) is our conduct and attitude to moral values in the course of the struggle to achieve working class power. I think it is not unfair to say that many Communists believe or appear to believe that under these conditions any action is morally justifiable which helps in the working class struggle or can be said to further the fight against capitalism . . .

For these values, these general principles—the sacredness of human life, truthfulness, pity—are not merely of enormous importance. They are the very values we are accused of ignoring, of trampling on. Our attitude towards *these* values constitutes the gravamen of the charge against us. It is with these then that we should begin. [John Shaw, June 1958.]

There is a type of Marxist ethical theory which can give rise to a cruelty, tryanny and untruthfulness which is indefensible. It is the theory which finds *no other* criterion of morality than victory in the class struggle. Marxists may be prevented from such conduct if they give full value to the general laws of morality, which, however, though authoritative are never absolute. . . . [John Lewis, June 1958.]

We may or may not find Communist ideas on ethics and morality adequate and acceptable. We cannot deny that Lenin and his followers genuinely sought a guide to action consistent with the fundamentals of Marxist belief. It may be argued that just as Stalin put Lenin's political thought into a straitjacket, so Lenin himself was responsible for putting into a straitjacket the authentically humanist elements in Marx's teaching.

To date the story of societies built upon Marxist-Leninist foundations can hardly be considered encouraging by thoughtful Communists not only concerned with socio-economic development but with truly human development too. It has tended to show that the belief that morality should be subordinated to the interests of the cause can, in a period of revolution and of the dictatorship of the proletariat, lead to an appalling misuse of power and to cruelty imposed in the name of Communism. Whether it is possible to evolve something different without weakening the revolutionary foundations of Marxism itself remains to be seen.

Meanwhile, like nations everywhere, those moving towards socialism under the leadership of the Communist Party require some sort of moral guidelines. The Soviet Union's code is spelt out in the most recent Programme of the Communist Party of the Soviet Union. A team of Russian Marxist political leaders and academics in 1968 summarised it thus:

> With the victory of socialism communist morality acquires all the necessary conditions to develop to the full. Characterising the essence and the tasks of the new morality Lenin said that it is based on the struggle for the *consolidation and completion of communism*. The ethical principles and standards of this new, genuinely humane morality are set down in the Programme of the C.P.S.U.
>
> The most important principles and features of communist morality are devotion to the communist cause, love for the socialist motherland, conscientious labour for the good of society, a high sense of public duty, revolutionary humanism and socialist internationalism. Communist morality presupposes consistent implementation of the principles of collectivism, comradely mutual assistance, friendship and

fraternity of all the peoples of the U.S.S.R., uncompromising attitude to all who violate public interests, and to the enemies of communism, peace and freedom of nations.[11]

This is little more than an elaboration of the concept that morality should be subordinate to the interests of Communism. It reflects little of Marx's concern for the individual in his own right.

A less simplistic approach to morality than that which we have been considering and which goes direct to Marx for its inspiration comes today from Communist-humanist philosophers like Maurice Cornforth. Yet, lacking any permanently valid code, even Cornforth is driven to conclude in his *Communism and Human Values* that until all exploitation of man by man is ended, 'morality cannot be based on a generalised human standpoint' but only on a class standpoint. For 'all the working classes' the 'practicability and human desirability of the aim demands and justifies the adoption of all those means of organised struggle which are necessary for attaining it.'

Which, after all, does little more than echo Lenin's dictum.

FURTHER READING
Chapter 4

William Ash, *Marxism and Moral Concepts*, New York: M. R. Press, 1964.

Santiago Carrillo, *Problems of Socialism Today*, London: Lawrence & Wishart, 1970.

Maurice Cornforth, *Communism and Human Values,* London: Lawrence & Wishart, 1972.

James Klugmann and Paul Oestreicher, ed., *What Kind of Revolution?*, London: Panther Books, 1968.

5 The Revolution and After

THE year 1848 in which the *Communist Manifesto* was published has gone down in history as the great year of revolutions. Around a score of revolutionary risings and insurrections occurred in Europe during the course of that single year. All were bloody. It is not surprising that when Marx and Engels wrote of revolution they most often thought of violent revolution.

In certain exceptional places and circumstances, they would sometimes concede, the qualitative change from one system to another, the transfer of political and economic power from one class to another, might just conceivably occur without the use of physical force. But they took it for granted that those who had everything to gain by the perpetuation of the status quo would most likely resist by violence any attempt at fundamental change.

Of all the Communist revolutions which have occurred to

date none has been peaceful. Communist parties in areas of the world where revolution is fairly obviously not on today's agenda tend now, however, to emphasise that it is not their intention to gain their ends by violence. They say that it should in the circumstances of today be possible to produce revolutionary change by peaceful means. If violence should come it will be from the other side, from those desperate to cling to their profits, place and power. Although this is not a fundamental departure from Marxism-Leninism it does represent a very significant shift in emphasis.

The British Communist Party, like the huge Italian Communist Party, has in recent years been moving away from the concept of a bloody struggle for power, which it accepted in the nineteen-twenties and thirties, towards the expressed belief, or at any rate the hope, that in British conditions 'this mass struggle for political power could be carried through by peaceful means, without civil war.'[1]

Its official programme, which with every new, revised edition over recent years has tended to move further away from advocacy of violent revolution, puts it like this:

> The struggle for political power will be intense, will go through many phases and take many forms. In the Parliamentary field the aim must be to win a Parliamentary majority, pledged to decisive socialist change and actively backed by the working people. Such a Parliament would be very different from what we have today.
>
> It will not be simple to achieve this. There will be advances and setbacks. Political power must be won; and in the struggle for power, the winning of a majority in Parliament, supreme organ of representative power, is one of the essential steps.[2]

What is visualised is a broad united front or alliance of the Left, backed by the militant working people, with the Communist Party as their revolutionary vanguard: 'When a socialist majority in Parliament is won it will need the support of the mass movement outside Parliament to uphold the decisions it has taken in Parliament.' Thus winning a parliamentary majority is but 'one of the essential steps'. Extra-parliamentary forces will be brought into action too. In certain circumstances, presumably, this could take the form of armed workers in the factories, and on the streets 'asserting the people's will' for which there is the Czechoslovak precedent of 1948.

Whether they would need to go into action (which would bring us back to the civil war situation), would depend upon the way in which the ruling class reacted. Where no one resists there is no one to fight. It takes two to make a war. But a struggle of some sort is visualised:

These developments, this programme, will have to be fought for by the mass movement at every step, with conscious understanding of the issues at stake. The ruling class will not easily surrender wealth and power. On the contrary, it will strive by every means, direct and indirect, constitutional and unconstitutional, to restrain and impede the popular movement, to break its strength or sap its unity. Against all such attempts popular vigilance and mass action will be essential.

The working class and popular movement will need to be ready to use its organised strength to prevent or defeat attempts at violence against it, its organisations or representatives, or other illegal actions by reactionary forces at home or by agents of their foreign allies.

There will be particular dangers of such resort to force

at crucial stages of the struggle, for instance when a general election is likely to result in a socialist majority; or even more when a socialist government has been returned and is taking essential measures to break the economic and political power of the monopolies.

The extent to which the popular movement, above all its working class core, is informed and vigilant, the extent to which it is geared to bring all its formidable strength into play in support of socialist policies, will be the decisive factor. This strength will determine whether the verdict is accepted, or whether, in defence of their interests, the capitalists resist by force.[3]

British Communists have not stepped very far out of line with Marx himself on this. Frederick Engels wrote: 'At least in Europe, England is the only country where the inevitable social revolution might be effected entirely by peaceful and legal means. He [Marx] certainly never forgot to add that he hardly expected the English ruling classes to submit, without a "pro-slavery rebellion", to this peaceful and legal revolution.'[4]

It will be seen that this is not a total rejection of violent revolution as such. Nor need it be since Marxists have never claimed to be pacifists. A wealthy, deeply-entrenched ruling class with much to lose might be expected to resist expropriation, by force of arms if necessary. Lenin almost certainly would have assumed that this would be so. Whether British Communists are today able or even willing to lead an armed struggle is beside the point. What we are here concerned with is to follow the logic of their argument to its legitimate conclusion.

It can be argued that if violence must be anticipated then the best form of defence is attack. It might therefore be essential to get in first with what the revolutionary government would hope was going to be the decisive blow. In which case there is still some validity in the frequently asserted belief that if you want Communism you must be prepared for civil war 'when the Red Revolution comes'.

Moscow has increasingly in recent years tended to play down the civil war element although, admittedly, it is not always easy to distinguish between propaganda intended to serve Russian foreign policy interests and what are genuine expectations and intentions.

Latin America is, one might think, the continent where violent revolution is most likely to come. There the need for the total transformation of social structures is real and urgent. In practice this means revolution of some sort—a proposition which is accepted by many Christians as well as Communists. The whole continent stands in urgent need of being propelled from a feudal, or semi-feudal, semi-colonial system into something more appropriate to the twentieth century. There is a small but immensely wealthy ruling class with all the levers of power in its hands. It has never shown any reluctance to use violence.

Even so, an imposing list of Russian academics, researchers and political leaders have put on record the official view that Latin American Communist parties might contemplate a 'peaceful road to socialism'. Here is what they say:

Moreover, favourable prerequisites for the peaceful development of the revolution already exist in a number of countries in Latin America. In those countries where it is less likely that the whole revolutionary process will develop peacefully, there are also possibilities for making broad use of the legal mass forms of struggle at specific stages of the revolution. This opportunity should be used to the maximum because it fully answers the interests of the people and will be constitutionally legal (and, consequently, will have a wider social basis) even if at subsequent phases of the revolutionary struggle the actions of the reaction will force the masses to take up arms.

Latin American Communists are proceeding from the fact that revolution is not synonymous with armed struggle. The principal thing in it is the transfer of power and ownership of the principal means and instruments of production from one class (or classes) to another. This can be achieved with or without resort to arms, depending on the existing conditions.[5]

This may look like so much eyewash—propaganda intended to fool political innocents. However, Moscow-orientated Communist parties have indeed opted out of the violent revolution in numerous Latin American countries in recent years, sometimes to the fury of their comrades in arms. They have abandoned guerrilla alliances in which they were playing a leading part, left their comrades in the field and attempted the hazardous enterprise of trying to filter back into open, constitutional action. For this they have been denounced as counter revolutionaries by other Marxist groups, just as were the French Communists during the 'student revolution' of May 1968.

The argument used in its defence by the French Communist Party is perhaps relevant here, the argument that to attempt revolution where no revolutionary situation exists is only to play into the hands of the enemies of Communism and to assist the coming to power of a dictatorial regime of the extreme Right.

Alternatively, since Latin American Communists were not long ago engaged in unsuccessful armed struggle, it may be that on the basis of that experience they feel that an attempt can and ought to be made to achieve a revolution by peaceful means.

At the moment of writing, a Left-wing coalition under President Allende of Chile is attempting to carry through a peaceful but total transformation of the social structure. Allende is a Marxist but not an orthodox Communist. The Communist Party of Chile supports him in his aim of a peaceful, though not necessarily gradual, progression from capitalism to some sort of Marxian socialism. Allende's is not a Communist revolution although it could with time become one; in which event the probability of violence coming from the old dominant class would presumably be increased. British Communists, in particular, watch the Chilean experiment with more than usual interest.

Communists should change with changing situations and in recent years many have shown themselves to be more flexible than in the past. But ultimately the Communist is, by the very nature of his beliefs, committed to revolution of some sort. About this there can be no doubt. As James Klugmann, British Communist Party theoretician put it:

> Lenin wrote in his 'Letters on Tactics' of April, 1917: 'The transfer of State power from one class to another *class* is the first, the principal, the basic sign of a *revolution*, both in the strictly scientific and in the practical political meaning of the term. [Lenin's italics.]
>
> This is the heart of the matter, the essence of revolution, and not the form of struggle, the degree of violence or non-violence, nor the mood nor even the intentions of those who participate.[6]

Lenin, of course, had a great deal to say about revolution and every good Marxist-Leninist knows much of it by heart. Indeed, Stalin declared that 'Leninism is the theory and tactics of the proletarian revolution in general, the theory and tactics of the dictatorship of the proletariat in particular.'[7]

Lenin held that what he called imperialism, the present, 'highest' or last stage of capitalism must lead to economic crisis, war, collapse, and so to popular uprisings if Communists played their part correctly. 'Imperialism is the eve of the Socialist Revolution' was his message.

He defined the revolutionary situation thus:

The fundamental law of revolution, confirmed by all revolutions and particularly by all three Russian revolutions in the twentieth century, is as follows: it is not sufficient for revolution that the exploited and oppressed masses understand the impossibility of living in the old way and demand changes; for revolution it is necessary that the exploiters should not be able to live and rule in the old way. Only when the 'lower classes' *do not want* the old and when the 'upper classes' cannot *continue in the old way* then only can the revolution be victorious. This truth may be expressed in other words: revolution is impossible without a national crisis affecting both the exploited and the exploiters.

It follows that for revolution it is essential, first, that a majority of the workers (or at least a majority of the class-conscious, thinking, politically active workers) should fully understand the necessity for revolution and be ready to sacrifice their lives for it; secondly, that the ruling classes be in a state of governmental crisis which draws even the most backward masses into politics . . .[8]

Marxism, he wrote, 'demands an attentive attitude to the

7

mass struggles in progress, which, as the movement develops, as the class consciousness of the masses grows, as economic and political crises become more acute, continually gives rise to new and more varied methods of defence and attack. Marxism, therefore, positively does not reject any form of struggle.'[9]

Following upon his experience of the 1905 revolution he foresaw the struggle ahead as taking the form of 'riots—demonstrations—street battles—detachments of a revolutionary army—such are the stages in the development of the popular uprising.'[10]

His comment on the Irish people's Easter Rising of 1916 is instructive since at the time he could not foresee that it would quickly lead on to something immensely bigger:

> The misfortune of the Irish is that they rose prematurely, when the European revolt of the proletariat had *not yet* matured. Capitalism is not so harmoniously built that the various springs of rebellion can immediately merge into one, of their own accord, without reverses and defeats. On the contrary, the very fact that revolts break out at different times and in different places and are of different kinds assures wide scope and depth to the general movement.
>
> Only in revolutionary movements which are often premature, partial, sporadic, and, therefore, unsuccessful, will the masses gain experience, acquire knowledge, gather strength, get to know their real leaders, the socialist proletarians, and in that way prepare for the general onslaught, in the same way as separate strikes, demonstrations, local and national, mutinies in the army, outbreaks among the peasantry, etc., prepared the way for the general onslaught in 1905.[11]

However, both Marx and Lenin emphasised that Communists should never 'play with revolution'. But when the revolutionary situation developed they should place themselves at the head of the masses leading them in a short, sharp struggle for power. If it failed, they should learn from the experience, see it as a dress rehearsal, then fight again, next time to win.

From the Russian experience of 1917, Communist parties tended to assume that this was a model capable of universal application. The Communist International, dominated as we have seen by the leaders of the Russian party, did the same:

> The October revolution overthrew the rule of the bourgeoisie. This victorious proletarian revolution expropriated the expropriators, took the means of production from the landlords and the capitalists, and for the first time in human history set up and consolidated the dictatorship of the proletariat in an enormous country. It brought into being a new, Soviet type of State and laid the foundations for the international proletarian revolution.[12]

Looking forward to a period when the revolutionary tide would be rising, the ruling classes disorganised and the masses in a state of revolutionary ferment, the *Programme* spelt out the need for a step-by-step build-up:

> This mass action includes: strikes; a combination of strikes and demonstrations; a combination of strikes and armed demonstrations and finally, the general strike conjointly with armed insurrection against the State power of the bourgeoisie. The latter form of struggle, which is the supreme form, must be conducted according to the rules of war. . . .[13]

And in the expectation that the predicted World War II

would offer opportunities similar to those which World War I presented to the Bolsheviks it said:

> The fundamental slogans of the Communist International in this connection must be the following: 'convert imperialist war into civil war'; defeat the 'home' imperialist government; defend the U.S.S.R. and the colonies by every possible means in the event of imperialist war against them.[14]

With hindsight one may say that this sounds somewhat different from the way things developed, and remote from how they are today. In the West, only Trotskyists, Maoists and other 'heretics' now talk like that. But it all seemed realistic enough to Communist Party members at the time.

Proletarians are mainly urban dwellers, so the seizure of power, it was assumed, would occur in the cities. The decisive struggle would most likely be in the capital city where political power resided. Thus it had been in Russia and thus, therefore, it would be elsewhere. It was, of course, purely theoretical because no successful Communist revolution occurred during the lifetime of the Comintern. There were peasant risings here and there as, for example, in the Philippines, and limited guerrilla war, including a 'long march' led by Luis Carlos Prestes in Brazil. But nowhere did the party have a chance to lead a proletarian revolution to victory.

It was only years later, after China had fallen to the Communists, that the writings and experience of Mao Tse-tung forced revolutionaries of every type, everywhere, to do a lot of hard new thinking.

FURTHER READING
Chapter 5

The British Road to Socialism, London: Communist Party of Great Britain, 1968.

Ernesto 'Che' Guevara, *Bolivian Diary*, Introduction by Fidel Castro, London: Jonathan Cape/Lorrimer, 1968.

Herbert Marcuse, *Soviet Marxism: A Critical Analysis*, New York: Vintage Books, Random House, 1961.

Ho Chi Minh, *On Revolution: Selected Writings 1920–66*, edited by Bernard B. Fall, New York: Signet Books, 1968.

William J. Pomeroy, ed., *Guerrilla Warfare and Marxism*, London: Lawrence & Wishart, 1969.

6 Whose State: Theirs or Ours?

WHAT follows the revolution? Since they might conceivably have to live through it, this is of greater importance to most people than are the details of what life would be like in some far and distant Communist society.

Between the conquest of power, which is the Communists' first goal, and Communism, which is their long-term one, lies a lengthy period, a whole epoch, throughout which the populace must live under what Marxists call the dictatorship of the proletariat. This is likely to be all that those who make the revolution will ever know if experience to date is anything to go by.

Marx and Engels wrote about it at some length. Lenin, for whom it became a matter of immediate and practical importance, put 'teeth' into their theories. What we have had in Russia for more than half a century, and now have in other Communist-ruled countries, has grown out of those theories which originated with Marx and Engels and upon which Lenin imposed his own particular stamp. Yet it satisfies relatively few Western Communists today.

The hard fact is that Communists have still to find an acceptable form of State organisation for that all-important transitional period between the proletarian revolution and the emergence of an authentically socialist society. So far, the 'socialism with a human face' of which Alexander Dubcek, ill-fated Prime Minister of Czechoslovakia, dreamed has still to materialise.

The Paris Commune of 1871, which was the first attempt to establish some sort of a modern Communist regime, was put down in blood. The French bourgeoisie took appalling revenge against the Communards, executing men, women and children in their thousands. But the experience was full of lessons for Marx and Engels.

It demonstrated that heroism is not enough. Revolutionaries must have clear goals. The violence of the French ruling class was indicative of the sort of reaction Communists must expect when they seriously threaten the property rights of the ruling class. The experience emphasised, too, that there could be no question of going straight from capitalism to Communism. There must be an intervening period during which some pretty rigid curbs would have to be put on liberty.

THE STATE

Political theorists had taught that the State stood above classes. It was representative of society as a whole. In the Paris of 1871 the full weight of the State machine was used against one class, the proletariat, by another, the bourgeoisie. And this, Marx concluded, was really no more than one must expect.

In capitalist society the State was a coercive power wielded in the interests of the property-owning class: 'an organisation of the possessing class for its protection against the non-possessing class.'[1]

On the eve of the October Revolution Lenin made a new study of the Paris Commune, and of the writings of Marx and Engels on the State. He used these to demonstrate that the immediate task ahead involved the breaking up of the existing State machine and the creation of an entirely new one. 'It is clear', he wrote, 'that the liberation of the oppressed class is impossible, not only without a violent revolution, but also without the destruction of the apparatus of State power which was created by the ruling class. . . .'[2]

Basing himself firmly on Marx and Engels, Lenin argued that the State was an instrument of the ruling class by means of which it maintained its rule. When it was not seriously threatened the ruling class could rely upon the 'weapons of persuasion': Parliament, the press and pulpit. When it was seriously threatened it resorted to use of 'the weapons of coercion'; the police, courts, judiciary and, in the last resort the standing army. A major task of the revolution must be to 'smash' the existing State machine and replace it with one which served the interests of the new ruling class, the proletariat. This would be the dictatorship of the proletariat: 'After the proletariat has won political power it must completely destroy the old State machine and replace it by a new one consisting of an organisation of the armed workers, after the type of the Commune.'[3]

Parliamentary democracy had been a fraud. '*Every* State is a machine for the suppression of one class by another. . . . The most *democratic* bourgeois republic is a machine for the oppression of the proletariat by the bourgeoisie.'[4] The dictatorship of the proletariat alone could emancipate humanity from the oppression of capital 'from the lies, falsehood and hypocrisy of bourgeois democracy—democracy *for the rich*— and establish democracy *for the poor*, that is, make the blessings of democracy *really* accessible to the workers and poor peasants.'[5] [Lenin's italics.]

The capitalist class used parliamentary democracy to maintain some semblance of peace, law and order, to manage its political affairs and to give those robbed of any economic power the illusion that they had a decisive say in determining their own destiny. But when the ruling class was seriously threatened it would not hesitate to replace democratic rule with a more open form of dictatorship.

PROLETARIAN DICTATORSHIP

After the revolution, the dictatorship the Communists would introduce would not be of the few against the many but of the many against the few. Bourgeois parliamentary democracy was a subtle, veiled form of dictatorship. The absence of economic democracy made it in any case very largely a sham.

But the dictatorship of the proletariat, i.e., the organisation of the vanguard of the oppressed as the ruling class for the purpose of crushing the oppressors, cannot result merely in an expansion of democracy. *Simultaneously* with an immense expansion of democracy which *for the first time* becomes democracy for the poor, the dictatorship of the proletariat imposes a series of restrictions on the freedom of the oppressors, the exploiters, the capitalists. We must crush them in order to free humanity from wage-slavery; their resistance must be broken by force; it is clear that where there is suppression there is also violence, there is no freedom, no democracy.[6]

As the country moved through socialism towards Communism and so towards the classless society, the need for such a dictatorship would be progressively reduced and so, also, would the need for the State itself.

The Marxist-Leninist teaching on the State provides a fascinating example of Marxist dialectical thinking. Here, indeed, is the unity and conflict of opposites. Greater freedom is reached by means of an openly proclaimed limitation of freedom; true democracy is achieved by way of dictatorship; the classless society is arrived at via the most open rule of one class over another which in time it totally eliminates; the State withers away only after a period in which it has been immensely strengthened.

No one who has studied Marxism-Leninism need be surprised that rigid control over legislature, press, pulpit, judiciary and the armed forces was imposed upon the people of the Soviet Union by the ruling Communist party. It was a legitimate interpretation, not a betrayal, of basic Marxist teaching.

What may at first glance seem surprising is that the dictatorship should have lasted so long. For the idea that those who made the revolution would live to see the country pass through the period of dictatorship to the greater freedom beyond seems to be implicit in much Marxist thought.

However, when one takes a closer look at the writings on the subject it is seen that this important question was left somewhat vague by the founding fathers of Marxism. For example Lenin could say:

> It requires a fairly long period of transition from capitalism to socialism, because the reorganisation of production is a difficult matter, and because the enormous force of habit of

running things in a petty-bourgeois and bourgeois way can only be overcome by a long and stubborn struggle. That is why Marx spoke of an entire period of the dictatorship of the proletariat as the period of transition from capitalism to socialism.[7]

'A fairly long period', 'a long and stubborn struggle', 'an entire period'. . . all in one paragraph!

On another occasion Lenin wrote: 'The dictatorship will become unnecessary when classes disappear.'[8]

This is not as simple, short and direct as might appear, for elsewhere Lenin writes:

> The abolition of classes means, not merely ousting the landowners and the capitalists—that is something we accomplished with comparative ease; it also means *abolishing the small commodity producers*, and they *cannot be ousted*, or crushed; we must *learn to live* with them. They can (and must) be transformed and re-educated only by means of very prolonged, slow, and cautious organisational work. . . . The dictatorship of the proletariat means a persistent struggle—bloody and bloodless, violent and peaceful, military and economic, educational and administrative— against the forces and traditions of the old society.[9]

More than half a century has passed since the dictatorship was established in Russia. Most of the men who made the revolution are long since buried. But the small commodity producers are still around. So too are the 'forces and traditions of the old society'. And so also is the dictatorship of the proletariat—quite legitimately on this showing.

But even this is not enough, for Lenin also wrote: 'The class of exploiters, the landowners and capitalists, has not disappeared and cannot disappear all at once under the dictatorship of the proletariat. The exploiters have been smashed, but not destroyed. They still have an international base in the form of international capital. . . .'[10]

Here and elsewhere Lenin would seem to be suggesting that the dictatorship must continue for so long as there is a capitalist 'international base' which may reasonably be construed to mean for as long as capitalism remains powerful anywhere. This is not a question of just playing with words; Russian Communist leaders and Leninists generally refer back to the original texts for their authority as a matter of course. And, the structure of the dictatorship of the proletariat, being what it is, it is the leaders, not the people, who decide how the texts should be interpreted.

Looking at the thing from the sidelines it would seem that maybe the Russian leaders had the founders of Marxism-Leninism on their side when they saw Dubcek as a liberal suffering from dangerous illusions!

Kim Il Sung, leader of the Communist Party in North Korea, has in recent years come to be seen as a Marxist-Leninist leader and thinker in his own right. His views on the role of the dictatorship of the proletariat were elaborated at length in what was described as an important article published in Pyongyang on 4 February 1971, and put out over North Korean radio on that date. The following are some typical passages from the article which are a 'hard-line', but quite legitimate, statement of Marxist-Leninist teachings on bourgeois democracy and on the dictatorship of the proletariat.

> Democracy as a political concept assumes a class character from the first and, consequently, there has been and there can be no super-class 'democracy' or 'pure democracy.'

Should there be any higher form of democracy than the proletarian dictatorship, it would be no longer democracy. . .

The dictatorship of the proletariat is the weapon of the class struggle and the weapon of the building of socialism and communism. Only by steadfastly maintaining the dictatorship of the proletariat and steadily strengthening it, can the working class win complete class and national liberation, successfully build socialism and communism, and perform its historical mission with credit. . .

As the reality shows, where the dictatorship of the proletariat is weakened and the social life is 'liberalised' and 'Westernised' through the import of reactionary bourgeois culture, the capitalist elements inevitably grow and the reactionary bourgeois trends and bourgeois fashion are fostered. This leads people to feel illusionary yearning for the bourgeois West, blind to the superiority of socialism. . .[11]

SOME PROBLEMS

Early in this century Rosa Luxemburg, leader of Germany's Left socialists, foresaw that Lenin's ruthless approach to party organisation and to the dictatorship of the proletariat could lead to trouble, more particularly because he insisted that the Communist Party as the vanguard of the proletariat would determine the nature and duration of the dictatorship. With the party's pyramidal structure this meant in effect that immense power must inevitably be placed in the hands of a small group of men at the apex of the pyramid. In practice this would be dictatorship by a few individuals at the most, not the dictatorship of a class.

This is exactly what happened in the Soviet Union and it has caused Communists the world over a great deal of trouble and some heart searching, as a consequence. One may argue that the Russian leaders should not have permitted so much power to pass into the hands of a single individual, Stalin; that there should have been collective leadership. Nonetheless, given the dictatorship of the proletariat as conceived by Marx and Engels, and the form of party organisation devised by Lenin, it is difficult to argue that the hideous things which happened during the Stalin era were just perversions, deviations and distortions for which Stalin alone was responsible. The risk was inbuilt. They were not accidental, they were already inherent in Marxist-Leninist thought.

Certainly, we should not, for example, be surprised at attempts to silence Pasternak, Sinyavsky, Daniel, Solzhenitsyn and others who are today operating in the field of ideas. This is what dictatorship of the proletariat as interpreted by Lenin is all about. It is of the essence that the 'weapons of persuasion' be kept firmly in the hands of the State until such time as the threats against it have ceased to be significant, and until the mass of the public have become proof against non- and anti-Communist ideas.

The political power of the local bourgeoisie may be quickly broken, the basis for its economic domination eroded over a relatively short period of years. But the 'ideological super-structure' which grew out of the capitalist system survives far longer. The dictatorship of the proletariat must continue at the very least until that superstructure has been eroded out of existence.

Capitalism has developed unevenly. Some countries to which Communist rule has come are more advanced than others. The tendency will be, therefore, for some to outstrip others as they move towards the desired point where the dictatorship is no longer required. Czechoslovakia was a case in point.

Because Czechoslovakia was politically years ahead of Tsarist Russia when Communist rule came, it was understandable that its people, led by its intellectuals, should find the dictatorship even more irksome than have the Russians; understandable, too, that its people should want to get back to the freedoms they knew in the pre-socialist period—freedoms which the Russians have never yet experienced. But with intellectuals in the U.S.S.R. already restive and pushing for greater freedom there was a danger that the Czech example might lead to the process getting out of hand. Insidious capitalist influences, slowly eliminated over the past half century, might start creeping back again and the work of the dictatorship of the proletariat be undone.

For, as we have noted, long after the old economic system has been destroyed 'bourgeois' ideas survive. The old corrupting influences born of an acquisitive society retain their potency. Arguing in Marxist-Leninist terms, if there is still a danger of their becoming active fifty years after the revolution, then this goes to prove how pernicious is the capitalist system itself. It is not so much evidence of some weakness in the Communist system as convincing proof that capitalism is even more sinister than was imagined.

Arguments such as these, incidentally, made it possible for Communists in the democratic countries of the West to accept during the nineteen-thirties the liquidation of Old Bolsheviks, the party purges, the hounding down of the 'enemies of Communism' whom Khrushchev was later to reveal were in most cases no more than those people Stalin feared as possible rivals.

Against all expectations, Communist rule had been established in a single country and socialist power was in the process of being consolidated despite the absence of any new round of successful revolutions elsewhere. But there were serious problems built into the Soviet situation. Under Stalin's leadership—or in response to his relentless drive—the people of a vast, backward country were being inspired, dragged and dragooned into erecting a twentieth-century industrial society. Since the first step on the road to industrialisation is the building up of heavy industry, production of consumer goods had to wait. Build up industry today and the goods would begin to flow from the factories into the shops tomorrow. It was a lengthy process and so long as it continued belts had to be drawn in.

Now, a nation can be induced to make huge sacrifices in time of war. Monotonous food, poor quality clothes and the general shortage of consumer goods may be accepted as part of the sacrifice required for victory. In order to be able to gain acceptance for such deprivations a war mentality must be created. If the emergency continues too long war weariness may set in.

Most wars are short by comparison with the period of time which was required to industrialise the Soviet Union. So government pressure on the public had to be built up over the years with persuasion and coercion going side by side, but with the greater emphasis necessarily having to be placed upon coercion. In the years between the revolution and World War II the mammoth task was attempted and to a great extent accomplished. But there was no comparable rise in the standard of living. Always, it seemed, it was a case of jam tomorrow, never jam today. And the promised hope of greater freedom diminished rather than grew.

There was another problem. 'Socialism in a single country' had been regarded as impossible. Stalin was attempting and achieving the impossible in the face of a hostile world, a world where the rulers of all the Great Powers spared no effort to sabotage the Soviet experiment.

Russia was surrounded by nests of spies. They were to be found in Riga, Shanghai and around the periphery of the Soviet Union. The imperialists had unlimited funds and would stop at nothing. If now they were succeeding in buying and corrupting even men who had suffered exile with Lenin and risked their lives in the revolution, then here was evidence indeed of the corrupting influence of capitalism. The dictatorship of the proletariat must continue and be even tougher than was expected.

The men who made the revolution, it had been supposed, would be the ones who would steer their people through the harsh transitional period into the greater freedom of socialism. Most of them, as it transpired, never lived to see this. Stalin had them shot.

Once the need for the dictatorship had continued for more than a generation legitimate doubts could be raised as to whether anyone would ever see the end of the dictatorship. For, as time went on, there came into existence a group, if not a class of men whose place, power and privilege derived from the dictatorship. They had a vested interest in its perpetuation and their sons and daughters who inherited privileged positions had an even greater interest in its continuance. Again, this basic weakness of Lenin's concept of the dictatorship was inbuilt.

These major flaws in the theory and practice of the founding fathers have become apparent as time has gone on. They have led to many people leaving the Communist Party. Equally significant, there are thoughtful Communists who today are troubled by them even though they remain within the party, and there are growing numbers of Marxists who can find no

8

political home except within the amorphous, unstructured movement of the New Left.

PRIVILEGED GROUPS

As long ago as 1934 Ignace Lepp, who had organised writers and intellectuals right across Europe on behalf of the Comintern, turned up as Professor of Philosophy at Tiflis University —in Stalin's home town. It was not long before Lepp found himself in a rarefied atmosphere a million miles from that in which the impoverished workers of Moscow and elsewhere lived. Lepp knew the price which was being paid by workers and peasants for the industrialisation programme. He knew the terrible sufferings which the masses were enduring—and from which millions in Russia materially benefit today—in the name of socialist construction. Intensive industrialisation had drained the countryside of much of its manpower. The meagre rations of the people were being cut ever further. And these had known little but privation ever since the revolution of 1917.

He was invited to a reception after giving a lecture. Lepp writes: 'It was then, with a sense of shock, that I saw being served, at this social gathering in Odessa, large quantities of caviare, butter, and other food hard to come by in Russia; vodka was flowing freely, and there was plenty of good wine from the Caucasus and Crimea.'[12] These were not foreigners being lavishly entertained for purposes of external propaganda. The local heads of the regime were having a blow-out among themselves.

Lepp was equally perturbed by the attitudes of the people in this new 'high society'. The women, in particular, were putting on airs and graces, flaunting furs and jewels which had been in fashion before the 1914 war. Men and women were drinking heavily and talking loudly with all the conceits typical of upstarts. Everyone talked contemptuously of workers and peasants; they were arrogant with their servants. These were the gilded few at the top.

Those who have read Alexander Solzhenitsyn's *The First Circle*, published more than thirty years after Lepp had his disillusioning experience, will recognise it all. There are the banquets given by the Prosecutor who had made a regular career out of those sent to their deaths or into exile by Stalin. The Prosecutor's wife, Alevtina, 'knew that a family needs to be well fed, that carpets and table linen are important status symbols and that cut glass is a fitting ornament for a dinner party. . . Tonight, in the bright light over the two long tables, the noble crystal flashed many-coloured sparks from all its diamond-cut facets. . . By half-past ten a score of dishes had been passed round . . . and the guests, crowded and getting in each other's way, made it their business not to eat but to talk amusingly and showed a studied contempt for the food. . .' And so on, and so on. . .

None of this is really surprising. It has much to do with ordinary human frailty, with greed, avarice, gluttony and love of power. But it has little to do with Communism. Significantly those who have been able to create for themselves such a way of life have, in the main, been the very ones who were expected to lead their people out of the dictatorship from which they, the gilded ones, derived their privileges.

This is, of course, only part of the picture. Side by side with it went fantastic industrial progress. The means of production remained socialised. 'Socialist construction' went ahead at a time when Western capitalism was stagnating. But it was bought at a price and it is only too easy to understand why the dictatorship drags on over the years.

One is entitled to doubt whether, with the best will in the world on the part of British, Italian and other 'liberalising', 'Westernising' Communists, the post-revolutionary period would be fundamentally very different in their respective countries from that in Russia, or whether it could last less long. True, there would not be the same necessity for ruthless industrialisation and, therefore, the pitiless drive of Stalin's Russia. Most of the other features of the local and world situation which are given as reasons for perpetuating the dictatorship are, however, likely to be present. This being so, they may be expected of necessity to bring a typically tough Marxist-Leninist response over an equally protracted, seemingless endless period of time.

A REVOLUTIONARY CRITIC

There was as we have noted one widely respected revolutionary socialist leader, Rosa Luxemburg, who foresaw the course that events might take. Like Lenin, Rosa Luxemburg was steeped in the writings of Marx and it was from her understanding of Marxism on the one hand and her humanity on the other that she came to believe that the course he was following might bring disaster to Communism. In particular it was the authoritarian elements in his thought and practice that alarmed her, especially as they took shape and form, first in his concept of a highly centralised, elitist party and later in the dictatorship of the proletariat.

Rosa Luxemburg was an exact contemporary of Lenin's, both being born in the year 1870. Brilliant daughter of a Jewish merchant in Russian Poland, she was an active revolutionary at the age of sixteen, a political exile by the time she was nineteen. In Switzerland she came to know Lenin, Plekhanov, the great Marxist theoretician, and other Russian revolutionaries in exile. They were endlessly arguing, writing, organising for the day when they could return home and contribute decisively in leading a socialist revolution. From them she learned, with them she shared her mind.

She moved on and in Germany she quickly became one of the leaders of the Left faction of the powerful Social Democratic Party. For years she thrashed out her ideas with men of the party's Centre and Right who were seen as the political and intellectual giants of the international socialist movement. The party prided itself on its early links with Marx and Engels but its more militant members held that it was already taking the sting out of Marxism by de-emphasising the class struggle and the need for revolution.

With Lenin she called for peace on the eve of World War I and when the war became a reality appealed to workers everywhere to oppose it. Her credentials as a revolutionary Marxist-Socialist were incontestable as Lenin's. But there were important areas of disagreement. In his booklets *What is to be Done?* and *One Step Forward Two Steps Back*, written in the early part of this century, Lenin argued his case for democratic centralism as the form of organisation required for a revolutionary Marxist party that really meant business.

This trend in Lenin's thinking alarmed Rosa Luxemburg and she became all the more deeply disturbed when she saw leading members of the Russian Social Democratic Party accepting Lenin's proposals. 'One Step Forward Two Steps Back', she wrote, 'is a methodical exposition of the ideas of the ultra-centralist tendency in the Russian movement. The viewpoint presented with incomparable vigour and logic in this book, is that of pitiless centralism.'[13]

Perceptively she wrote: 'If we assume the viewpoint claimed as his own by Lenin . . . we can conceive of no greater danger to the Russian party than Lenin's plan of organisation.' Then, in italics throughout, she went on: 'Nothing will more surely enslave a young labour movement to an intellectual elite hungry for power than this bureaucratic straitjacket, which will immobilise the movement and turn it into an automaton manipulated by a Central Committee.'[14]

When the Russian Revolution came in 1917 Rosa was in jail. She gained knowledge of it only from newspaper clippings brought to her by visitors to her cell. Even so she flashed warning lights, by means of writings smuggled out to her supporters.

Already she could see that her earlier fears were being confirmed. In her booklet *The Russian Revolution* written in early 1919 she deplored the sheer lack of socialist principle that Lenin and his comrades were showing in their dealings with the peasants, with the people of other nationalities within the old Tsarist empire, and in the elimination of democracy which was occurring in the name of the dictatorship of the proletariat. Against this she counterposed 'the active, untrammelled, energetic political life of the broadest masses of the people'.[15]

The dictatorship of the proletariat, she argued, should be something much richer, more creative than Lenin's idea of it—'the bourgeois state which is an instrument of oppression of the working class stood on its head'. It should rest on the political training and education of the entire mass of the people. 'Freedom only for the supporters of the government, only for the members of one party—however numerous they may be—is no freedom at all.'[16]

Socialism by its very nature could not be decreed or introduced by *ukase*. Lenin was completely mistaken in the means he employed to maintain 'indispensably necessary' public control: 'Decree, dictatorial force of the factory overseer, draconic penalties, rule by terror—all these things are but palliatives. The only way to a rebirth is the school of public life itself, the most unlimited, the broadest democracy and public opinion. It is rule by terror which demoralises.'[17]

Prophetically, she continued:

... with the repression of political life in the land as a whole, life in the soviets must also become more and more crippled. Without general elections, without unrestricted freedom of press and assembly, without a free struggle of opinion, life dies out in every public institution, becomes a mere semblance of life, in which only the bureaucracy ramains as the active element. Public life gradually falls asleep, a few dozen party leaders of inexhaustible energy and boundless experience direct and rule... Yes, we can go even further: such conditions must inevitably cause a brutalisation of public life: attempted assassinations, shooting of hostages, etc.[18]

Rosa Luxemburg did not jib at the use of the word 'dictatorship' but she saw the proletarian dictatorship as something very different from that conceived of by Lenin:

Yes, dictatorship! But this dictatorship consists in the *manner of applying democracy*, not in its *elimination*, [Rosa Luxemburg's italics] in energetic, resolute attacks upon the well entrenched rights and economic relationships of bourgeois society, without which a socialist transformation cannot be accomplished. But this dictatorship must be the work of the *class* and not of a little leading minority in the name of the class—that is, it must proceed step by step out of the active participation of the masses; it must be under their direct influence, subjected to the control of complete public activity; it must arise out of the growing political training of the mass of the people.

Rosa Luxemburg made due allowances for the difficulties experienced by the Bolsheviks—that, for example, they had had to proceed 'under the frightful compulsion of the world war, the German occupation and all the abnormal difficulties connected therewith, things which were inevitably bound to distort any socialist policy, however imbued it might be with the best intentions and the finest principles.'[19]

She continued: 'The danger begins only when they make a virtue of necessity and want to freeze into a complete theoretical system all the tactics forced upon them by these fatal circumstances and want to recommend them to the international proletariat as the model of socialist tactics.'[20]

This, of course, is exactly what happened. But Rosa Luxemburg did not live to see it. She was released from prison, but a few weeks later was re-arrested. On her way back to jail after questioning, she was seized by a group of Prussian officers who smashed her skull with their rifle butts. Half-dead she was taken a short distance in a car, finished off with a revolver shot at point blank range. Her corpse was flung into the Landwehr Canal. Her writings were banned in Communist circles throughout the Stalin era, her name rarely mentioned. It is only recently that she has been partially and posthumously reinstated in Communist circles. But it is not difficult to see why she has today a growing following among the New Left who take what they want from Marxism and reject precisely those features of Lenin's theories and practice to which she years ago first drew attention.

FRAGMENTATION

It was the centralism, to which Rosa Luxenburg objected, that led to the first serious rift in the international Communist ranks and so to today's growing fragmentation of the movement. Unlike Lenin, Rosa Luxemburg had not, of course, to administer the dictatorship of the proletariat. She was detached from it, looking at it from the sidelines or, more accurately, through the bars of her prison cell. Whether her view of what the dictatorship should be like was a practicable one has never yet been put to the test. But there can be no doubt that she put her finger on what have been shown to be its most disturbing features.

Lenin saw the infant Soviet government as the vanguard of the world revolution. So did Trotsky. Contrary to their expectations the world revolution did not come, yet the Soviet State succeeded in surviving nonetheless. As rulers of the Workers' Fatherland and bosses of the sole ruling Communist Party, the Russian leaders insisted over the years that all other Communist parties must follow their pattern even though conditions and traditions might be very unlike Russia's.

Through the medium of the Third International (Comintern) they imposed their will upon the rest, not only dictating forms of organisation and policies but promoting and demoting leaders, too. By a happy twist of history Russia had been the first to 'go Communist', so they made the most of it, clearly enjoying the exercise of power which this brought them. With every party of necessity marching in step with the C.P.S.U. the world Communist movement had the appearance of being united, monolithic.

Largely for tactical reasons, Stalin dissolved the Comintern during World War II. Foreseeably, this made it more difficult for the artificial unity of the past to be maintained. However, for the time being the rest of the revolutionary army kept marching in step more or less from force of habit.

A new situation was created with Russia's occupation of so much of Eastern and Central Europe at the end of the war. No longer was there just one Communist regime. There were now other ruling Communist parties on the international scene. The new governments might be Russian puppets, their Communist leaders Russia's clients, but they still ranked as rulers in their own countries.

For years the Communists had dreamed of one big U.S.S.R., one big happy family of nations. Grouped around Russia, yet autonomous; working out their own destinies whilst helping each other as comrades in the same movement.

According to traditional Marxist thinking, Communism should be adapted to the different traditions and cultures of these various nations. Stalin himself had said as much in his book *Marxism and the National and Colonial Question*. But that was long ago. Now he tried to impose the Russian pattern upon each of the new Communist States just as had been done with the various Communist parties linked to the old Comintern. This was not too difficult since it was the Russian Red Army, not the local Communists who, in most cases, had overthrown the old capitalist or fascist regimes. And it was thanks to the Red Army and its guns that the new regimes continued to exist.

Yugoslavia was different. Alone among the new ruling parties the Yugoslavs and Albanians could claim that in guerrilla war they had by their own sacrifices and force of arms overthrown the old ruling class and established Communist rule. Moreover, it was not without importance that neither had a common frontier with the U.S.S.R.

Stalin tried to impose his pattern on Yugoslavia but its independent-minded leader Tito refused to knuckle under. Overnight Tito became a fascist. He was denounced as such not only by the Russian leaders but by those of every other Communist party too. He and his party were expelled into the outer darkness. No one supposed he could survive.

When Tito took aid from the West, Communists elsewhere were convinced that even if, against all their confident predictions, he continued to exist it could only be by leading his country back to capitalism. Instead, he set about trying to prove in practical fashion and with some success that there were other roads than the Russian one which Communists might follow. That the dictatorship of the proletariat, about which Lenin and Stalin had been so dogmatic, might differ in some respects in different countries, and the socialist goal still be reached.

With Stalin's death and the gradual easing of tensions, more tolerable relations have been established between Yugoslavia and the Soviet Union. As time has gone on, Tito's way of doing things has exerted its own particular influence on Marxists elsewhere, yet not so much upon the traditional Communist parties as upon some of the growing number of people who hold that in being Marxists they need not necessarily accept the whole of Lenin, and that still less need they be Stalinists.

Yugoslavia's experiments in workers' control have had some interesting repercussions. There were, for example, the Clyde shipyard workers in Scotland whose determined efforts in 1971 to keep the yards going after they had been declared redundant aroused widespread interest. Yugoslav attempts to spread power and responsibility at the level of 'ordinary' working people, bringing them into decision making, and harnessing their initiative, are welcomed by many of today's new Marxist Left. They see these as encouraging indications that it may be possible to evolve a form of Marxist socialism which is a viable alternative to the Russian type with its excessive concentration of power at the top. They see it also as being in accord with the needs of a modern technological society for which the old hierarchical system, typical of both capitalist and Communist countries to date, is not necessarily the best. Vertical hierarchies have been typical of bureaucracy. But the mindless obedience demanded of the worker both under capitalism and in Soviet Russia, is little suited to today's highly developed industry. In Yugoslavia the vertical chain of industrial command is increasingly replaced by ground-level participation. Workers make real decisions. Titoism in this respect may be more 'modern', more relevant to the needs of a socialist society moving into a technological age.

Historically, probably the most important thing about Tito's break with Soviet Communism is that it started a process of schism and fragmentation. This continues to spread so that anyone who today talks, for example, of 'the international Communist conspiracy', the 'Sino-Soviet bloc' or the 'Communist monolith' tends to sound like a political troglodyte.

There are precedents for this process of fragmentation. The period of the Reformation is one. This demonstrated that when a split occurs in a monolithic body it is likely to be quickly followed by a process of fragmentation with new sects and 'churches' springing up left, right and centre. Heretics tend to continue to be heretics, thinking up new heresies. Rebels tend to continue to rebel. One split leads to another.

FURTHER READING
Chapter 6

Ken Coates and Tony Topham, ed., *Workers' Control*, London: Panther Books, 1970.

Milovan Djilas, *The New Class*, London: Thames and Hudson, 1957.

Milovan Djilas, *Conversations with Stalin*, London: Rupert Hart-Davis, 1962.

Frederick Engels, *The Origin of the Family, Private Property and the State*, London: Lawrence & Wishart, 1940.

Frank Jellinek, *The Paris Commune of 1871*, London: Victor Gollancz, 1937.

Robert Looker, ed., *Rosa Luxemburg: Selected Political Writings*, London: Jonathan Cape, 1972.

Georg Lukács, *History and Class Consciousness*, London: Merlin Press, 1971.

Rosa Luxemburg, *The Russian Revolution and Leninism or Marxism?* Ann Arbor, University of Michigan Press, 1961.

Rosa Luxemburg, *The Mass Strike, The Political Party and The Trade Unions*, Colombo, Ceylon: Young Socialist Publications, 1964.

Rosa Luxemburg, *Social Reform or Revolution*, London: Merlin Press, (undated).

7 Maoists and Fidelistas

WHILST Stalin was preoccupied with driving Tito out of the Communist family and then trying to destroy him and his detested regime a bigger, immensely more devastating split was developing. The huge Communist Party of China after a generation of fighting was completing the conquest and consolidation of power. And it was doing so along lines not at all according to the Marxist-Leninist pattern.

No one with any knowledge of China and its people could for one moment have imagined that the Chinese would, or even could, for ever slavishly copy Russia or, for that matter, be the puppet of any other country either. Stalin nonetheless proceeded to treat the Chinese much as he had the smaller nations of Eastern Europe, and demanded the same response. Sending in limited technical aid, plant and technicians would, he seemed to suppose, create a new dependence upon the Soviet Union and so ensure that China would tread the Russian road. Nothing of the sort happened.

From the very beginning of its life the Chinese Communist Party had taken its own course. It continued to do so. More important for the purposes of this study of contemporary Communism than the issues which finally brought about the formal split are the distinctive teachings of Mao Tse-tung and the means by which the Chinese Communist Party came to power. The first, the teachings of Mao, have led to rival Communist parties springing up and challenging the traditional parties right across the world. The second, the means used, has set a new pattern for the seizure of power from which guerrilla fighters of all sorts in each of the developing continents learn much today.

For years on end Communists under the leadership of Mao Tse-tung maintained an unremitting struggle for power. Sometimes it took the form of guerrilla warfare, sometimes the Communists joined with the 'enemy' nationalist, Kuomintang forces in the fight against the Japanese—most often having their greatest successes when operating behind the Japanese lines. And as time went on their struggle took the form of all-out revolutionary war.

Strangely, one might think, this did not cause the Russian leaders (who never really approved of Mao Tse-tung and his comrades in any case), the Comintern or Communist parties elsewhere to revise their thinking on the subject of the armed struggle. They still went on writing and talking in the old terms just as though the Chinese experience, meaningful though it was for the whole of the colonial and semi-colonial world, just did not exist. Still less were they influenced by the fact that it ran counter to almost everything recently written by Marxists on the struggle for power.

The Chinese party's long drawn out fight was valued for the contribution it made to the Allies' war against the Japanese end of the Berlin-Rome-Tokyo axis. The heroism and endurance of the Chinese comrades were quoted in Communist propaganda as inspiring examples to be followed. Their martyrs, along with those who died at the hands of German Nazi and Italian fascist torturers, stiffened the resolve of Communists elsewhere to prepare themselves for any sacrifice the coming revolution might demand of them. But they did not change their thinking about the nature and form of revolution.

The Chinese experience grew out of the situation into which the party was born. 'In China, without armed struggle the proletariat and the Communist party could not win any place for themselves or accomplish any revolutionary task', wrote Mao Tse-tung. It was certainly the case that in the old China little was left for the party but the armed struggle. It was brought into existence in a turbulent period in China's history. Illegal from the day of its inception, it had from the first to use violence to make any headway at all.

In the first days after the formation of the party in 1920 it was reasonable to talk as Mao did of the 'proletariat and Communist party', coupling them together. For, following the established Marxist pattern the Communists concentrated their main attention on the cities, recruiting and leading workers in strikes and, more particularly, students in bloody battles with the police. The young Mao was himself active in both these areas despite his petty bourgeois-peasant origins. The expectation was that the workers, supported by the students, would be able to lead risings in the towns and that these would fan the whole country into flames. The risings were ruthlessly crushed, and the harassment, persecution and torture which followed obliged the leaders to do some serious re-thinking.

Until then the Marxist message had been that the seizure of power should be short and sharp, as in Russia. In China, however, the initial failure in the towns proved to be no sort of Russian 1905 dress rehearsal. Instead the repression and counter-revolution gradually led the Communist leaders to decide that they had no alternative but rural guerrilla warfare, based on the countryside. They and their revolution could be crushed in the cities. The vast rural areas with their thousands of villages provided bases from which the cities could in due course be surrounded and assailed. Thus the emphasis changed from urban to rural conflict.

Small pieces of territory were seized and held for as long as was militarily possible. Sometimes these had to be relinquished when the pressure upon them became too great but, since they were small so, too, were the defeats. The Red bases which were established as time went on were able to merge like so many oil spots on a table cloth, joining up until they covered whole areas. Again, the first inclination was to follow Russia's example. Chinese soviets were established in the South with their own government and constitution. Repeated extermination campaigns finally led Mao and his comrades to abandon the whole area which had come under their rule and to embark on the epic Long March to the North.

MAO AND ARMED STRUGGLE

In all, the armed struggle covered a period of almost thirty years. For more than twenty of these Mao's was the dominant influence. He had of necessity to be both a political and a military leader. Like the good guerrilla leader that he was, he kept the political goals, immediate and long-term, always in the forefront of the picture. The two aspects of the struggle went inseparably side by side.

9

The armed struggle was 'arduous' and 'protracted'—two words which constantly crop up in Mao's writings and in the vocabulary of Maoists everywhere today. The struggle could hardly have been more varied, taking different forms as the situation changed and developed. There was the early armed defence against repression; establishment and defence of a soviet State within the non-Communist one; resistance to counter-revolution; united front collaboration with the Kuomintang nationalist government. And, in a different period, anti-government guerrilla activity against the Kuomintang, conducted in the mountains, forests, swamps and open plains; opposition to foreign invaders during the Sino-Japanese War; guerrilla warfare growing into revolutionary warfare, then positional warfare in the fight against the Japanese during the Pacific War. Then, subsequently, in the post-war period, the triumphant last show-down with Chiang Kai-shek. And so to final victory.

In short, the Chinese experience of the conquest of power coming only at the end of protracted struggle was the exact opposite of that of the Soviet Union and also that hitherto taken for granted by the Comintern. Mao's secretary Chen Po-ta, who in 1966 was to be one of the leaders of the cultural revolution, summed up the Chinese experience like this:

> The conclusion to wage a protracted revolutionary war in the villages, use them to encircle and then take the cities; the conclusion to establish and maintain revolutionary power in many small bases and gradually develop and expand these bases through prolonged struggles until seizing power throughout the country—these clear-cut conclusions were reached by Mao Tse-tung over twenty years ago by applying Marxism-Leninism in his study of

the problems of the Chinese revolution. They are new, Marxist conclusions arrived at in a colonial and semi-colonial country. These new conclusions are correct because they have been verified by the Chinese revolution and because they are being verified by realities in the countries of South East Asia.[1]

The 'realities' in the countries of South-east Asia to which Chen referred were the adherence to the old 'short, sharp struggle for power' concept which led to the defeat of numerous Communist risings in the area. The sole exception, or partial exception, was Indo-China, where Ho Chi-minh modelled his strategy upon Mao Tse-tung's and so succeeded in establishing Communist power in North Vietnam.

Summarising, one may say that the distinctive features of Mao's contribution to Marxist thought on the practice of revolution are:

1. 'A single spark can start a prairie fire.' A revolutionary army can be built up from small beginnings over a long period of time with the seizure of power coming at the end of a protracted and arduous struggle. But the revolution must be fought with the gun.

2. In semi-feudal, semi-colonial countries the most appropriate form of struggle may not be the traditional short, sharp insurrection by the proletariat in the cities. It may take the form of guerrilla warfare conducted in the countryside, with villages used as bases, and in which the purpose is ultimately to surround the cities from the countryside.

3. Thus, whilst it is acknowledged that it is the historic mission of the proletariat to provide the main drive in the building of socialism, in the struggle for the conquest of power the peasantry can play a leading role.

No matter what ritual noises may, therefore, be made by Maoists, in practice Mao's teachings on revolution turn upside down traditional Communist thought on the key question of how the revolution should be fought.

MAO'S MARXISM

Mao may not be a Marxist philosopher of the front rank but he has made his own very distinctive contribution to current Marxist thought. Ever practical, he has drawn upon those aspects of Marxism-Leninism which are of greatest usefulness to him in his efforts to launch his country on the road to Communism whilst simultaneously raising it from its despised semi-colonial, semi-feudal status to take its place in the forefront of the nations of the modern world. In particular, he has seized upon the Marxist doctrine of 'contradictions', the struggle of opposites, and used this with breathtaking audacity, consciously introducing and harnessing conflict to force the pace of change and development in industry, education, the State, even within the Communist Party itself.

'There is nothing that does not contain contradiction; without contradiction there would be no world',[2] Mao says. And so, suiting the action to the word, he has based many of his policies on the belief that contradictions continue to exist within socialist society and, this being so, must be turned to good account.

Some naïve ideas seem to suggest that contradictions no longer exist in a socialist society. To deny the existence of contradictions is to deny dialectics. The contradictions in various societies differ in character, as do the forms of their solution, but society at all times develops through continual contradictions. Socialist society also develops through contradictions between the productive forces and the conditions of production.

In a socialist or communist society, technical innovations and improvement in the social system inevitably continue to take place; otherwise the development of society would come to a standstill and society could no longer advance . . . the existence of contradictions between the individual and the collective in a socialist society is nothing strange. . .[3]

Always, Mao's approach has tended to be more audacious than that of 'orthodox' Communists of the West. In this case, one might think, it is more logical and intellectually honest too. Marxist-Leninists have paid lip service over the years to the continuance of the dialectical process, with its law of the interpenetration of opposites, within socialist society. They have, however, generally behaved as though conflict ceased to play a dynamic role with the consolidation of socialist power.

Applying the dialectic to his own society at this stage of its development, Mao distinguishes between 'contradictions between ourselves and the enemy' and 'contradictions among the people'. These two types of social contradictions, he says, are totally different in nature. Contradictions 'between ourselves and our enemies' he defines as 'antagonistic' ones. Those within the ranks of the working people are 'non-antagonistic'.

In the latter category he includes the following: contradictions within the working class, peasantry, intelligentsia; contradictions between the working class and the peasantry, the working class and other sections of the working people on the one hand and the national bourgeoisie on the other, contradictions within the national bourgeoisie.

Although Mao may be a Stalinist in some respects he goes much further than anyone would have dared to do in Stalin's Russia when he acknowledges, and then suits the action to the word, that 'certain contradictions do exist between the government and the masses. These include contradictions between the interests of the State, collective interests, and individual interests; between democracy and centralism; between those in positions of leadership and the led; and contradictions arising from the bureaucratic practices of certain State functionaries in their relations with the masses.'4

All these conflicting interests can be used for positive ends since development comes through conflict. So at the time of the Cultural Revolution and the Red Guards he dared to do what no other Communist leader had done: he consciously and deliberately gave free rein to conflict within the State bureaucracy, the educational system and, even more remarkable, within the party itself in order to assist the country's progress towards socialism. Mao certainly takes his dialectics seriously, not only as a philosophy of change but as the means by which one cooperates with and uses the process of change and development to achieve Communist aims.

MAOIST PARTIES

Once Mao's writings and exploits became known outside China, the erosion of the Soviet leaders' authority within the world Communist movement was almost inevitable. Acceptance of Mao's teachings helped to make Peking be seen, in the Third World in particular, as an alternative to Moscow. Within Communist parties everywhere there were people who were very soon taking as much and more from Mao as from Stalin.

These in many cases became founding members of new,

Maoist Communist parties—rivals to the traditional ones—which were formally established once the Moscow-Peking split had occurred. Most often these parties have added the title 'Marxist-Leninist' to their names suggesting by implication that they are the 'true believers', the others the 'heretics'.

Heretics, it is said, isolate certain doctrines from the main body of the faith, then place undue emphasis upon them. This is what other Communists in effect, though in non-theological terms, say the Maoists have done. Be that as it may, Maoists everywhere tend to be distinguished by narrowness and rigidity in the interpretation they give to their Marxism.

An extreme seriousness of approach, accompanied by a certain puritanism, characterises China's Communists. This seems also to be the hallmark of most of Mao's followers outside of China. 'Sectarian' is the word which other Communists use for them. By this they mean that the Maoists keep themselves apart from the mainstream of Left politics, have a 'more Marxist than thou' attitude to other Marxists, enter into few alliances of any sort and are critical of everyone but the leaders in Peking.

With the intolerance of the extreme dogmatist and armed with their copies of *Quotations from Chairman Mao Tse-tung*, they pursue their own austere way, disciplined, dedicated, utterly convinced of the correctness of their cause and giving unquestioning loyalty to Chairman Mao. Inevitably a movement such as this attracts to itself a certain type of follower who, though ready and eager to suffer martyrdom for his cause, nonetheless mechanically applies his beliefs 'according to the book' to every situation.

It was this that gained for them during the early days of the French student revolution of May 1968 a mixture of admiration and exasperation from their fellow students.

Admiration for their courage and self-discipline, exasperation at their tendency to go off on their own, little red book in hand, to do their own thing—which meant, to apply to the France of the late sixties what Chairman Mao said was good for the China of the thirties.

This exclusiveness, combined with a tendency to try to outdo each other with proofs of revolutionary fervour has also frequently led to the fragmentation of their own movement so that by now it is not at all unusual to find within a single country numerous Maoist organisations each claiming to be the one and only authentic voice of Chairman Mao.

One sees this 'sectarianism' at its most extreme in Ireland. There Communism has had little appeal. Yet, alone among Western Maoists, Ireland's have, despite dissensions and divisions, tended to make more impact than has the traditional Communist party. One may speculate that this may not be unrelated to the fact that they are products of a culture in which purity of doctrine and a certain austerity in the presentation of religion have been characteristic. The transition from past over-reliance upon a small, green *Catechism* embodying all the basic doctrines, to the *Little Red Book* has not perhaps been as difficult as might appear at first glance.

Typical of the Maoist approach was a call by one of the Dublin leaders for the 'peasants' of Northern Ireland to surround its cities from the countryside, just as China's peasants had done before them. It happens that no farmer in the North would regard it as anything but an insult to be called a peasant; and the conditions in the little area behind the Border are such that rural guerrilla warfare would be entirely inappropriate—although its city ghettoes offer almost ideal conditions for urban guerrillas.

Immensely more significant are India's Maoist and semi-

Maoist parties. The old-established Communist Party of India split at the time of the Sino-Indian border dispute of 1962. Some of its members followed the official line of supporting the Nehru Government, the argument being that it was 'benevolently neutral' in the cold war and relatively progressive in its domestic policies. Others claimed that Marxists should in all circumstances oppose their own government if it is in conflict with a Communist one. This latter group broke away to form the Communist Party of India (Marxist). They are now popularly known as the 'Marxist Party'.

These pro-Peking Communists were obviously the more uncompromising and revolutionary-minded, so it was not long before another split occurred. This time it was over the question of whether the C.P.I.(M) should collaborate in coalitions with non-Communist parties in day-to-day activities and more especially, in coalition governments. The new breakaway group, calling themselves the Communist Party of India (Marxist-Leninist) base their views and policies even more firmly and dogmatically upon the true doctrine of Chairman Mao.

Thus there were by now three competing C.P.I.s, with the Marxists and the Marxist-Leninists trying to outdo each other in practical evidence of their own militancy. In numerous parts of India, particularly in Calcutta, they have come into murderous conflict with each other bringing a sickening train of reprisal and counter-reprisal to the Indian political scene.

In 1969, primitive, land-hungry peasants attempting to seize land at Naxalbari, in the Darjeeling District on India's northern border, clashed with landlords' agents and police, with casualties on both sides. Members of the C.P.I.(M.L.) quickly moved in on the situation with the enthusiastic support of Radio

Peking and of the *Peking Review*, (foremost international Maoist weekly, published under Chinese Government auspices).

Soon the example of the Naxalites was being followed in half a dozen Indian States, often spontaneously but always with the Maoists leading and making the movement their own. Their message to the peasants was that in the primitive conditions in which these armed clashes occurred it was not necessary to be equipped with anything more than 'traditional' weapons. By this they meant knives, spears, bows and arrows. Nor was it necessary to have any previous knowledge of armed struggle. Using one of the sayings of Chairman Mao the Naxalites told the peasants and tribesmen that they should 'learn warfare from warfare', and gain more sophisticated weapons together with the necessary experience as they went along.

The Naxalites, with Peking's encouragement, have acted in the belief that Mao's 'a single spark can start a prairie fire' could prove true not only of China but of India too. China's radio network has from the start supported the movement stage by stage, with appropriate, carefully selected slogans taken from the sayings of Mao Tse-tung. The aim has clearly been to spread the flames as widely as possible.

Landless peasants have been encouraged to seize the land of which they have been deprived and then to kill—usually by beheading—any representatives of the landlords or the law who intervene. There has invariably followed the predictable, massive official over-reaction of the type which has so often helped rebel movements elsewhere: punishment of the entire local community, leading to mass support for the rebels and to the establishment of a revolutionary 'base' with its own local defence corps which in turn becomes yet one more guerrilla unit ready to link up with others elsewhere.

This technique used by the Naxalites is clearly seen by Peking as the prototype for revolutionary growth points in the Third World's forgotten areas.

For years delegations visiting Peking from Africa, Asia and Latin America have been told: 'What we have done, you can do.' Now they can also be given the more recent and often more relevant example of the Naxalites as well. For there are few countries in the developing continents which do not have their ethnic, religious or language minority groups, forgotten people, living in neglected areas which most frequently happen also to be ideal guerrilla terrain.

Communists who took their lead from Marx, Engels, Lenin and Stalin in the past assumed that the revolution would start in the urban centres and be led by the advance guard of the industrial proletariat. Today, those who follow Mao Tse-tung are more likely to put their hopes in the most primitive groups living far from the centres of power.

Whatever the future significance of these Maoist activities may prove to be, it is already the case that they help Maoists living elsewhere to feel that they are part of an international, truly revolutionary army which is already engaged in battle in decisively important areas of conflict. Subjectively, no doubt, they feel much as did members of the traditional Communist parties in the heady days of the twenties and thirties.

DIFFERENCES

Modelling themselves on Chairman Mao, the Maoists are characterised by the audacity of their thought and practice. To them the compromises which the traditional parties have made in recent years are so many betrayals. To them, quite simply, the 'revisionists' have sold out to the imperialists:

Firstly, because they now talk of the possibility of pursuing

peaceful roads to socialism whereas the only way is that of
the gun.

Secondly, because they are prepared to enter bourgeois
parliaments, to play the parliamentary game. This has been
denounced by the Chinese as 'parliamentary cretinism', since
violent revolution is a 'universal law' for the proletariat.[5]

Thirdly, because they have geared in with Russia's peaceful
coexistence policy, accepting the unmarxist proposition that
world war can and must be eliminated in the nuclear age.

Fourthly, because, just as Russia has disengaged from revolutionary commitment in many parts of the world so also
have the traditional Communists—which leads to their
playing a treacherous, counter-revolutionary role within the
working-class movement.

IN INDUSTRY

One early side-effect of publication of the *Selected Works of
Mao Tse-tung* in Western countries was that there was a
change of tactics used by many trade unions, particularly those
under Communist leadership. New ways of fighting the
bosses were discovered.

For example, the 'guerrilla' strike appeared on the industrial
scene. Instead of taking on employers in all-out battle involving
a mass withdrawal of labour the union would select strategically important enterprises, or departments within a single
enterprise, in which to stage one-day strikes, sit-ins or go-slows.
These, whilst cumulatively just as disruptive and costly to the
employer as would be a mass strike, are immensely less costly
to the workers and their unions. 'Guerrilla' strikes are, as it
were, the industrial equivalent of ambushes in which small
groups of guerrillas are used at strategically decisive points as
opposed to regular warfare involving large numbers of troops.

Quotes from Mao which influenced industrial thinking were taken straight from his military writings: 'We defeat the many with the few—this we say to all the rulers of China. Yet we also defeat the few with the many—this we say to the separate units of the enemy forces that we meet on the battlefield.'

Another of Mao's famous 'thoughts' adapted to industrial situations has been his famous sixteen-word formula: 'Enemy advances, we retreat; enemy halts, we harass; enemy tires, we attack; enemy retreats, we pursue.'

CUBA AND INSTANT REVOLUTION

Knowing little if anything about the guerrilla theories of Chairman Mao Tse-tung, Che Guevara, the young Latin American Marxist doctor of medicine, was also led by hard experience to the conclusion that the revolutionary struggle in a developing country can begin in the countryside and end in the city.

Che and his leader and comrade-in-arms, Dr Fidel Castro, started with the idea that the Cuban revolution should begin in the capital, Havana. They arrived on the shores of Cuba from Mexico on 2 December 1956, with a party totalling just eighty-two romantic revolutionaries. Government forces had been alerted and were waiting for them. They were immediately reduced to a mere dozen. Twelve men to make a revolution. This was indeed remote from the classical Marxian concept of how it should be done.

The handful of survivors had no choice but to take to the hills. Splitting into two tiny, hunted groups, one of seven and the other of five, they aroused the peasants in the mountains. Before long they had stirred great areas of the countryside with their dash and heroism. In the best guerrilla tradition they armed themselves at the expense of the enemy in frequent ambushes but relatively few direct confrontations. Aided by growing support in the cities they brought the vicious Batista dictatorship toppling down and seized the reins of government. It was all over in little more than two years. On 8 January 1959, Castro and Guevara with their colourful, bearded warriors made a triumphal entry into Havana.

Here was a stirring epic comparable to, though very different from, Mao's Long March. Here, too, was peculiarly convincing proof that in the Third World you do not have to wait for the revolutionary moment. You make your own revolutionary situation by simultaneously rousing the rural people, wearing down the government's armed forces, establishing support bases in the cities, eroding the economy of the country, and undermining the political power of the ruling class. In the end you have very largely yourselves created Lenin's revolutionary situation: the government is no longer able to govern and the people are united in their hostility to it.

Che's message was one of hope; strong, intoxicating stuff for impatient revolutionaries—and revolutionaries are almost by definition young men in a hurry. In capsulated form it went like this:

There is no reason why the armed struggle should not begin wherever you have suitable terrain, a handful of determined revolutionaries, access to sufficient arms to stage your first ambush (after which you arm yourselves with guns and ammunition taken from dead and wounded enemy forces) and a willingness to go into battle right away. Instant revolution.

In the book *Guerrilla Warfare*, Che Guevara lists 'three fundamental conclusions about armed revolution':

1. Popular forces can win a war against an army.

2. One does not necessarily have to wait for a revolutionary situation to arise; it can be created.

3. In the under-developed countries of the Americas, rural areas are the best battlefields for revolution.[6]

These 'fundamental conclusions' were born out of Cuba's very special situation and the unique circumstances in which the revolution was staged. Nonetheless they were presented by Castro and Guevara as being capable of universal application. As a Minister in government, Che Guevara was soon telling visiting delegations from Asia and Africa as well as from all over Latin America, that the message was applicable to their situations too. It was understandable that the revolutionaries among them went on their way rejoicing. Here was news to gladden the heart of any rebel.

Its appeal to Third World revolutionaries is obvious. It was less obvious, perhaps, that Che's teaching would influence the thought of Marxist revolutionaries in the 'affluent' countries too, so that there is by now an unmistakable Cuban imprint on certain areas of their thinking and, to a lesser extent, on the methods they use. Above all else the Cuban revolution helped to create a mood among members of the New Left which has had its repercussions in universities and colleges where conditions could hardly be less similar to those of a Spanish American Caribbean island.

Cuban Communism has its own special appeal at a variety of different levels of which the strictly political one may not necessarily be the most significant. After fifty years of grim, long-coated Soviet leaders and drably dressed Russian women pictured against a background of snow and ice, it comes as something of a relief to see the struggle for Communism at last being enacted in a setting of sunshine and flowers, by jaunty men and vivacious, beautiful girls. Cuban Communism has just that 'zing' that the Russian variety has so notably lacked.

The attraction of Communist Cuba has been greatly increased by its big neighbour's well publicised but unsuccessful attempts to strangle the little revolutionary regime. Here is a classic example of top dog and under-dog. The U.S.A. is the big, cowardly bully, Cuba the plucky little fellow who refuses to be put down. Very much in favour of the Cuban leaders is the fact that after a shaky start they managed to avoid letting their country become the puppet of either Russia or China. They have retained a fair degree of independence and gone pretty much their own way.

This helps to explain their particular appeal to the young and more especially to a generation which tends with some justification to distrust Great Powers and to identify much more easily with their victims.

The fact that Che left the position of power he had won, turned his back on the perks which come from office to return to the perils of guerrilla warfare in an attempt to start a continental revolution, and died in action, puts his name among the 'greats' for many who know little of Marx. That his illstarred Bolivian campaign defied many of his own rules and disproved many of his guerrilla theories is of less import-ance than that, as a wounded prisoner, he was secretly executed with the connivance of the C.I.A.

Here is a man who lived for the revolution. He sacrificed himself for it, turning his back on place and power; he suffered for it by choosing to endure once more the hardships of jungle warfare even though he knew that he was a very sick man. And he gave his life for his cause. This is what matters. And it has much to tell us about the spiritual needs of the younger generation in the materialistic West. More, perhaps, than it has to tell us about Cuba's revolutionary regime.

A generation which has for its heroes Che Guevara, Patrice Lumumba, Malcolm X and Martin Luther King, each dedicated to his own particular cause, and each murdered by his opponents, has no more lost its need for belief than it has lost its dreams.

It was a twist given to Che Guevara's message by his friend Regis Debray, the young French intellectual and writer on guerrilla warfare, that helped Western university revolutionaries to more easily apply it to their own situation. The key to Guevara-type guerrilla strategy is, Debray insisted, the *foco*, a 'Red base', small but of decisive importance, dependent upon the support of the local people for its continued existence. Such bases established at points vital to the enemy can spell his ultimate defeat.

Adapted to the advanced technological industrial society of the West the strategy takes the form of working to convert certain decisively important industries and enterprises into *foci*. The universities are tackled in this way too. For they today produce the scientists, technicians and others upon whom the whole industrial complex depends. And, of almost equal importance, they turn out 'engineers of acceptance'—products of political and social science departments whose work makes acceptable to the public a system which would otherwise be rejected as unacceptable.

The role of the revolutionary in the university is, therefore, according to this reasoning, to disrupt the university itself, and to turn it into a Red base. The worker's and technician's role is to do the same in enterprises vital to the industrial-military complex. Thus may the two pillars upon which the present system rests ultimately be brought down.

Presented in this form Che's message is one of 'instant revolution' for the cities of the world as well as for its

10

'villages'; as relevant to the student, university lecturer, technician or worker of Europe or the United States as to the peasant of South America.

The impact of the Cuban revolution upon Latin America was immediate, with numerous attempts in various parts of the continent to put Guevara's teachings into practice. Few of the *foci* which were brought into existence, in Venezuela, Peru, Colombia, Bolivia, Honduras, Guatemala and elsewhere, have managed to survive. Most have been ruthlessly crushed by government or else fragmented by differences which have arisen among the various Marxist groups which composed them. Despite this the appeal of Che Guevara and of Cuban Communism continues to exert its own particular influence upon Communists of the non-Communist world and upon others who are interested in revolutionary change.

BLACK POWER

The concept of the *foco*, in which a minority of committed, totally dedicated revolutionaries raises the revolutionary consciousness of the whole of the people around it, has taken firm hold in the Black Power movement of the United States. So, too, has Mao's concept of the Third World surrounding the 'cities of the world'. America's black population is at one and the same time at the very heart of the most important 'city' and is yet also part of the Third World.

The black ghetto has, they reason, all the features of a colony. It is a territory into which people of a different ethnic origin and culture come to establish commercial and trading enterprises. These derive their income from the local populace whom they shamelessly exploit for their own purposes, syphoning off the profits to invest outside the 'colony'. The white capitalists are the colonisers, the black public the colonised. Thus their situation makes them part of the Third World even though they dwell in the United States of America. This being so, the black people must be made conscious of their identity of interest with nationalist freedom fighters and Marxist revolutionaries in Asia, Africa and Latin America who are in open conflict with the imperialists.

As Black Power leader, Stokely Carmichael, puts it, the people of Asia, Africa and Latin America are their brothers. 'We can become, and are becoming, a disruptive force in the flow of services, goods and capital. While we disrupt internally and aim for the eye of the octopus, we are hoping that our brothers are disrupting externally to sever the tentacles of the U.S.'[7]

Here is an example of non-Communists taking what they want from Cuba and China whilst specifically rejecting Marx. 'The society we seek to build among black people', Carmichael declares, 'is not an oppressive capitalist society. Capitalism, by its very nature, cannot create structures free from exploitation.' He goes on:

> We are going to extend our fight internationally and we are going to hook up with the Third World. It is the only salvation—we are fighting to save our humanity. We are indeed fighting to save the humanity of the world, which the West has failed miserably in being able to preserve. And the fight must be waged from the Third World. There will be new speakers. They will be Che, they will be Mao, they will be Fanon. You can have Rousseau, you can have Marx, you can even have the great libertarian John Stuart Mill.[8]

This same approach is to be found among leaders of the American Black Panthers. Panther activist Joudon Major

Ford of Harlem, New York, interviewed by George Murray, Minister of Education of the Black Panther Party, says:

> We recognise the fact that we are a colony within the United States. . . So when we say that we have a colonial status within the country we mean that each separate community is a colony that is exploited just as South Vietnam, Algeria or Cuba were exploited by the imperialists. . . So that is part of our colonial thesis. We maintain that we are colonial slaves . . . and that we must also engage in an armed struggle as the Cubans engaged in armed struggle.[9]

And Ford reflected an attitude which is very much of this period when he went on to say that 'we will move in all revolutionary directions to destroy our enemy, regardless of the personal hang-ups of some people.' It would have been very difficult to find this approach in the nineteen-thirties when people of the Left normally identified themselves with one specific group or another.

To note that Mao and Che have influenced the thought of Black Power and Black Panthers is not to suggest that these are therefore 'Communist'. It is possible today to express agreement with Mao's dictum that 'political power flows from the barrel of a gun' and to accept that the Third World is the natural ally of revolutionaries who operate within the imperialist strongholds and yet not qualify for the Communist-Marxist label.

The number of people who accept some part or parts of Marxism without having any formal commitment to Communism must by now far exceed those who are organised Communists of one persuasion or another. With the appearance on the scene of rival schools of Communist thought, and with Stalin and Stalinism still hanging like millstones round the necks of traditional Communist parties, increasing numbers of young people now take what they want from Marxism without feeling any obligation to accept the doctrine in its entirety.

Having been taken from the West to Asia, Africa and Latin America, Marxism is now feeding back again in the form of new, less dogmatic thinking[10] which makes its own impact on the wider revolutionary movement. So also do the young churches of the mission continents make their impact on that very European entity that was once called Christendom.

FURTHER READING
Chapter 7

Stokeley Carmichael and Charles V. Hamilton, *Black Power: The Politics of Liberation in America*, New York: Vintage Books, Random House, 1967.

Fidel Castro and Regis Debray, *On Trial*, London: Lorrimer, 1968.

Eldridge Cleaver, *Soul on Ice*, New York: Dell, 1968.

David Cooper, ed., *The Dialectics of Liberation*, London: Penguin Books, 1968.

Regis Debray, *Revolution in the Revolution?*, New York & London: M.R. Press, 1967.

Frantz Fanon, *The Wretched of the Earth*, London: Penguin, 1967.

John Gerassi, ed., *Venceremos! The Speeches and Writings of Che Guevara*, London: Panther, 1969.

Ernesto 'Che' Guevara, *Socialism and Man in Cuba*, London: Stage I, 1968.

Ernesto 'Che' Guevara, *Reminiscences of the Cuban Revolutionary War*, London: M.R. Press/Allen and Unwin, 1968.

William Hinton, *Fanshen: A Documentary of Revolution in a Chinese Village*, New York & London: M.R. Press, 1966.

Lin Piao, *Long Live the People's War!*, Peking: Foreign Languages Press, 1965.

Mao Tse-tung and Che Guevara, *Guerrilla Warfare*, London: Cassell, 1963.

Mao Tse-tung, *Selected Works* (4 volumes), London: Lawrence & Wishart, 1954–1956.

Mao Tse-tung, *Selected Military Writings*, Peking: Foreign Languages Press, 1963.

Jan Myrdal, *Report from a Chinese Village*, London: Penguin Books, 1967.

Stuart R. Schram, *The Political Thought of Mao Tse-tung*, London: Penguin Books, 1969.

The Origin and Development of the Differences between the Leadership of the C.P.S.U. and Ourselves, Peking: Foreign Languages Press, 1963.

8 Conflict and Dialogue

L EON Trotsky of the cruel tongue and brilliant mind died
 an exile in Mexico, with an ice-axe in his skull. The
assassin was, it is believed, an agent of Stalin's. If we seek for
motivation we must find it in the diseased mind of the man
who in addition to effectively getting all power within Russia
into his hands claimed the right to determine every detail of
Marxist doctrine for the international Communist movement.
Trotskyism might yet be an ideological threat to Stalin,
therefore Trotsky had to die.

Trotsky no longer represented any sort of domestic threat
to Stalin. Any supporter he ever had in the Soviet Union had
long since been either executed or broken and sent into exile.
On the world scene, his Fourth International added up to very
little.

There were Trotskyist groups in many lands but none was
of any great significance and the overwhelming majority were

tiny even by comparison with the traditional Communist
parties few of which, in the world of pre-World War II,
themselves mustered more than a few thousand members. In
Spain, during the early days of the Civil War, the Trotskyists
had their own, separate fighting force, the POUM, which
insisted on trying to make Communist revolution whilst
others fought for the life of the Republic. The price the
Trotskyists paid for thus 'objectively aiding Franco' was all-out
military attack led by the Communist Party of Spain. And
Trotskyists the world over for the next thirty years were
branded by the Communists as pro-fascists—with the 'pro-'
conveniently omitted as often as not.

Some of the hatred felt for them sprang directly from their
ill-timed action in Spain. But there was, and continues to be,
another element which feeds it over the years. It is this: ever
since the Popular Front days of the nineteen-thirties—when
the Communist parties made so many concessions to Socialists
and Liberals in the interests of short-term though vital goals—
the Trotskyists have appeared to be playing the role once
played by the Communist parties themselves. In Britain, as
in so many other countries, they are the Communist Party's
only serious rivals for leadership of the militant Left in industry.

The Trotskyist is the militant of militants, the irreconcilable
revolutionary, the uncompromising, undeviating Marxist
purist. Not for him the deals with the reformers of capitalism,
the weighing up of pros and cons before going into strike
action in industry or guerrilla action in the Third World. He
is for direct action at 'the point of production': in the factories,
depots, mines, wherever the proletariat, vanguard of the
revolution, are to be found.

When Latin American Communist parties withdraw their
guerrilla fighters from the mountains, telling them to abandon

the armed struggle because the situation now calls for constitutional struggle and a peaceful road to socialism, the Trotskyists cry 'treason' and carry on the fight, if need be alone. Doctrinaire and aggressively certain that they alone interpret Marx's revolutionary message correctly, they claim the right to denounce the traditional Communists as Stalinists and traitors, to infiltrate social-democratic parties, work for the old-type 'united front from below' whilst simultaneously spurning as allies all but those who share their views. In other words, they do all the things that Communist parties did in their early, 'sectarian' days, uninhibited by any accepted restraints. For them the issues are still clear-cut and simple.

'A means', wrote Trotsky, 'can be justified only by its end. But the end in its turn needs to be justified. From the Marxist point of view, which expresses the historical interests of the proletariat, the end is justified if it leads to increasing the power of man over nature and to the abolition of the power of man over man.'[1]

Their war-cry is 'permanent revolution' and their aim is to make this a reality even though the smallness of their numbers denies them any real opportunity to influence events to any decisive extent. For them it is enough that he could write: 'The permanent revolution, in the sense which Marx attached to this concept, means a revolution which makes no compromise with any single form of class rule . . .' and that his life and death bore testimony to this belief.

In Mexico, and still more in Ceylon, there are, curiously, 'revisionist' Trotskyist parties which have acquired mass followings. In Ceylon these even play the constitutional game and turn up in coalition governments. One such, which included both Trotskyists and Communist Party, in 1971 found itself with an ultra-left insurrection on its hands. Calling themselves 'Guevarists', the young insurgents, among them many students, drew inspiration from Kim Il Sung and the Naxalites too.

Trotskyists first became of significance—though only of limited and mainly local significance—in Britain after Russia was brought into World War II. Since Hitler's attack upon the Soviet Union had made the war a 'just' one, the Communist Party, from opposing it switched to all-out support for the war effort. This became most meaningful in the war industries where Communist shop stewards were soon leading the workers in great production drives, giving the effort to increase the flow of arms all that they normally gave to the class struggle in terms of dynamism, leadership and untiring effort.

The Trotskyists at once jumped into the militant industrial leadership vacuum, working for strikes wherever they could and in some cases getting them. Since industrial grievances and injustices continue regardless of just and unjust wars, they were here and there able to gain a reputation for being the only true defenders of working class interests come what might. They have to this day retained something of this among certain groups of workers and have acquired it amongst others as a consequence of their willingness to call for and lead strikes almost regardless of either the circumstances or the chances of success.

Typical of those who hive off to the Left of the traditional Communist parties, the Trotskyists are fragmented into innumerable warring parties, groups and factions so that it is almost impossible to say at any given moment just how many there are or what they are currently calling themselves. In Britain and the United States there are normally not less than half a dozen, with two or three of these simultaneously claiming to be the true, authentically recognised affiliated party of the Fourth International. In Ireland where organised Trotskyists normally add up to scores rather than hundreds, there are, at the time of writing, three or four rival groups even within Dublin's relatively small student body.

They differ over their interpretation of Trotsky's message, particularly as concretised in the shape of current tactics. They share his name and, in broad terms, his belief that the attempt to build socialism in one country, Russia, led only to the betrayal of Communism and the establishing of State capitalism there; above all else, they share his belief in 'permanent revolution'.

This idea, which they find so attractive, was not Trotsky's alone. It was shared by Lenin. But Lenin had come to recognise before his death that, contrary to expectation, rivalries between European imperialist powers had not created the conditions in which the proletariat elsewhere could follow the Soviet example. In spite of this, Russia's revolution in fact survived. The Bolsheviks in the circumstances had no alternative but to press on alone towards their socialist goal using the peasants as allies in the task of socialist construction.

Trotsky maintained that the conflicting interests of workers and peasants within Russia, and the imperialist opposition from without, must render impossible the building of socialism in the one country. He continued to maintain this after Stalin had committed himself to going it alone. Since events stubbornly refused to proceed according to the classical Marxist rules, Trotsky held that someone must be betraying something, somewhere.

The Trotskyists and Stalinists of the capitalist countries still disagree as to whether Russia has, indeed, followed a socialist path or whether, as Trotsky maintained, she has ended up with nothing better than a form of State capitalism fraudulently represented to the workers of the world as a socialist society.

Trotskyists argue that because he followed a course contrary to Marxist teaching, Stalin betrayed the proletarian revolution and proletarian dictatorship, landing Russia with a State bureaucracy which degenerated into a personal dictatorship. 'One can understand the acts of Stalin', Trotsky wrote, 'only by starting out from the conditions of existence of the new privileged stratum, greedy for power, greedy for material comforts, apprehensive for its positions, fearing the masses, and mortally hating all opposition.'[2]

This, one may feel, is not unreasonable criticism of the nightmare aspects of the Stalin era, except, that is, that Trotsky was himself frequently charged with having strong 'Bonapartist' tendencies. And it is difficult to see how, had he been in Stalin's place, he could have done other than proceed with the attempt to build socialism in Russia once the Bolsheviks had successfully seized power and then, to their dismay, discovered that against all the Marxist rules, others were not doing the same. The historic process misfired on the one occasion when it was seriously put to the Marxist-Leninist test and Trotsky himself acknowledged this when he wrote:

This is the first time in history that a state resulting from a workers' revolution has existed. The stages through which it must go are nowhere written down. It is true that the theoreticians and creators of the Soviet Union hoped that the completely transparent and flexible Soviet system would permit the State peacefully to transform itself, dissolve, and die away in correspondence with the stages of the economic and cultural evolution of society. Here again, however, life proved more complicated than theory anticipated.[3]

Those last seven words might be taken as an epigram on the story of Communism in our day. That their founder from the start warned of where Stalinism would lead enables the Trotskyists to claim the right to take up a 'we told you so' attitude. There may be few signs of the permanent revolution in the West but there is nowadays sufficient armed struggle at any given moment in Latin America, Asia and Africa to lend credence to their claim that even though it is not occurring where Trotsky expected it, and although peasants rather than the proletariat usually do the fighting, it is a reality nonetheless.

It is characteristic of this present period that many students and militant young workers organised in the International Socialists, Young Socialists and similar bodies, or who take their inspiration from such papers as *Black Dwarf* and *Red Mole*, draw upon Trotsky's teachings without usually feeling any compulsion to join Trotskyist parties as such. Their number almost certainly exceeds that of the total membership of the various formally constituted Trotskyist organisations.

Trotsky to them is a symbol of the uncompromising, irreconcilable revolutionary. He is the man who rejected with contempt existing capitalist and Communist establishments alike. They read with approval his description of the permanent revolution as 'a revolution which makes no compromise with any single form of class rule'[4] and accept that his life and death bore testimony to this belief.

Current trends in the 'old', traditional Communist parties of Britain, Italy, U.S.A. and France provide all the evidence they need that the old gang have abandoned class struggle and proletarian revolution for a policy of class collaboration and counter-revolutionary opportunism.

CHRISTIAN-MARXIST DIALOGUE

The gulf between the traditional Communists and the Trotskyists is perhaps to be seen at its widest in the dialogue with Christian theologians which Communist leaders and scholars have been prepared to embark upon in recent years. Such dialogue is anathema to Trotskyists.

The willingness of Christians and Communists to find points at which minds meet and where it is possible to talk a common language reflects a recognition on both sides that a qualitative change has occurred in the world situation, and that this calls for a qualitative change in approaches and attitudes.

Both are undergoing an agonising process of renewal and in so doing they are alike reacting—or responding—to the changed world situation. Cold-war confrontations are hardly consistent with peaceful coexistence. Frozen 'Christian' attitudes have to thaw, Stalinist rigidity must yield to openness. Roger Garaudy may have been right when he told the Pierre Teilhard de Chardin Association in London that a crusade between two fanatisicms in the present state of the techniques of destruction could mean the annihilation of mankind.

By the time that the full implications of Khrushchev's speech at the Twentieth Congress of the Communist Party of the Soviet Union, 1956, had percolated through to Communist parties of the West, the World Council of Churches, and soon after this, the Catholic Church, were seeking to disengage from the cold war. Commitment to one half of a divided world against the other was hardly consistent with the claim to be a universal Church. The document *Gaudium et*

Spes which came from the Second Vatican Council declared: 'For our part the desire for dialogue excludes no one. . . We include those who oppress the Church and harass her in manifold ways.'[5]

And in his encyclical *Pacem in Terris*, Pope John XXIII wrote: 'Meetings and agreements, in the various sectors of daily life, between believers and those who do not believe or believe insufficiently because they adhere to error, can be occasions for discovering truth and paying homage to it.'

It was this sort of approach coming from both Christians and Western Communist leaders which provided and continues to provide grounds for authentic dialogue. It is absolutely basic to the whole concept of dialogue that fundamental differences between Christians and Marxists are not brushed under the carpet but admitted. This, paradoxically, forms the starting point for a meeting of minds. At a 'Marxism and Religion' conference in 1967, James Klugmann, editor of the British Communist Party's *Marxism Today* declared: '. . . we should, from the beginning, recognise (and respect) our differences of approach. For the dialogue to be fruitful we should no more hide our atheism than Christians their belief in God.'

Hyman Lumer, writing on 'Action and Ideology' in the American Communist Party's journal *Political Affairs*, July 1966, said: 'Co-operation and dialogue can no more be made conditional upon Communists giving up their atheism than it can upon Christians giving up their belief in God.'

Protestant and Catholic theologians and philosophers on the one hand and Marxist thinkers from traditional Communist parties, on the other, continue to meet year by year. It remains as difficult as ever to see how one can be a good Christian and a good Marxist-Leninist at one and the same time.

A being only considers himself independent when he stands on his own feet; and he only stands on his own feet when he owes his existence to himself. A man who lives by the grace of another regards himself as a dependent being. But I live completely by the grace of another if I owe him not only the sustenance of my life, but if he has, moreover, *created* my *life*—if he is the *source* of my life. . .[6]

No Christian-Marxist synthesis has emerged nor is this intended. Those dialoguing had first to understand each other's definitions. Even so, the conversations have been worthwhile. Here and there joint action has been attempted and experience shows that this is least likely to turn sour where both sides eschew the temptation to use such encounters as opportunities for proselytising.

Traditionally, Christians have been more concerned with the individual than with social change whilst Communists have been more preoccupied with social change than with the individual. It is here that dialogue may have most to offer— in enabling the two sides to explore what they have to learn from each other, although in the process Christians have already learned how much the Church has to say on the need for social change, whilst Communists have discovered how much Marx wrote on the individual.

A potentially promising field for dialogue would appear to lie in the relatively recently rediscovered interest in Marx's early writings on alienation.

MARX'S THEORY OF ALIENATION

Marx's theory of alienation has been taken up by thoughtful Communist Party members, Marxists and others of the New Left as being peculiarly relevant to our present situation. It has also been the means by which many on the Left have been introduced to Hegel, sometimes directly through Marx, in other instances via the works of the 'metaphysical Marxist' Herbert Marcuse whose *Reason and Revolution*[7] has revealed for many just how great was Marx's indebtedness to Hegel. Stalin held that Marx 'turned Hegel upside down' but the evidence suggests that the young Marx did much more than this. He took over and significantly developed many of Hegel's ideas, most significant of all for today being those relating to the predicament of alienated man.

Ever since the mid-fifties when alienation first became a vogue word, a spate of collections and selections from the writings of the young Marx has been appearing from publishing houses in the West and the U.S.S.R. These served to create a new awareness of Marx's early interest in the subject and a fascinated realisation of how much he has to say on it.

This in turn led to a belated recognition that the preoccupation with man's estrangement from himself, his work and society which provided the first dynamic for Marx's labours, runs like a single thread through all the years of his adult life. As a young man Marx was primarily occupied with philosophical aspects of the problem whereas in later life he devoted most of his time to studies in the economic field but he was throughout inspired by the desire to discover the why and wherefore of human alienation.

Most of his writings on the subject lay for a century unpublished, unregarded and unread. Even so, sufficient was available for Communists to concern themselves with the problem had they so desired. For example, *Wage-Labour and Capital*, which was amongst the most read and discussed of his writings, contains a passage that puts much of the theory of alienation in a nutshell:

11

But the exercise of labour power, labour, is the worker's own life-activity, the manifestation of his own life. And this life-activity he sells to another person in order to secure the necessary means of subsistence. Thus his life-activity is for him only a means to enable him to exist. He works in order to live. He does not even reckon labour as part of his life, it is rather a sacrifice of his life. It is a commodity which he has made over to another. Hence, also, the product of his activity is not the object of his activity. . . And the worker, who for twelve hours weaves, spins, drills, turns, builds, shovels, breaks stones, carries loads, etc.—does he consider this twelve hours' weaving, spinning, drilling, turning, building, shovelling, stone-breaking as a manifestation of his life, as life? On the contrary, life begins for him where this activity ceases, at table, in the public house, in bed. The twelve hours' labour, on the other hand, has no meaning for him as weaving, spinning, drilling, etc., but as earnings which bring him to the table, to the public house, into bed.

Alienation reached its peak in capitalist society where men are estranged from themselves, their work and their fellows, and everyone and everything is reduced to a saleable commodity. For its origins the Marxist goes back to the time when human history may be said to have begun, to the moment when man distinguished himself from the animal. Achieving his humanity by applying his labour to matter he thereby began for the first time to play some conscious part in controlling his own destiny.

But it was this very step forward—a qualitative change if ever there was one—which led to his beginning the ascent from the primitive tribal Communism—that first 'classless society—which had of necessity been his. The invention of tools and weapons made possible settled cultivation and more efficient methods. These led to the creation of a surplus of goods, and so to a situation where some men could appropriate that surplus, claiming it as their own private property. They could then use it, and the work of others, for their own enrichment. Thus was opened the way to exploitation and division of labour and with these the creation of a class society, divided into exploited and exploiters and resting firmly on the exploitation of human labour.

Work, human labour, is for the Marxist the means by which man creates himself as man and makes his own history. By his activity he realises and expresses his humanity. But it is also the means by which he creates something that in time comes to have domination over him. When primitive men fashioned for themselves idols, these things which they made with their own hands came in time to exert an independent influence upon them by determining and controlling their thoughts and actions. The idol-worshipper was enslaved by an object of his own creation. It took on, as it were, a separate existence apart from, outside the man himself, exercising domination over him. He was thus estranged, or 'alienated' from and by a product of his own work.

The life of capitalist man may not be controlled by graven images of his own making—although the golden calf has still all too much reality—but he is controlled and manipulated by, for example, market trends which are the product of human labour. So, too, with the worker at the machine: 'No special sagacity is required in order to understand that, beginning with free labour or wage-labour for example, which arose after the abolition of slavery, machines can only develop in opposition to living labour, as a hostile power and alien property, i.e. they must, as capital, oppose the worker.'[8]

In capitalist society, men are alienated at every level of society, with the working class the most alienated of all. 'The alienation of the worker in his product means not only that his labour becomes an object, assumes an *external* existence, but that it exists independently, *outside himself*, and alien to him, and that it stands opposed to him as an autonomous power. The life which he has given to the object sets itself against him as an alien and hostile force.'[9] The worker spends his days making things not for the joy of labour, self-expression and creativity, nor even for his own use. He works at machines the operation of which calls for little creativity on his part, and derives few human satisfactions from his labours.

His work is not the satisfaction of a need 'but only a *means* for the satisfaction of wants outside it.'[10] And the products of his labour serve to increase the power of capital and thereby to strengthen its hold over himself. He is the victim of something of his own creation.

> What constitutes the alienation of labour? First, that the work is *external* to the worker, that it is not part of his nature; and that, consequently, he does not fulfil himself in his work but denies himself, has a feeling of misery rather than well-being, does not develop freely his mental and physical energies but is physically exhausted and mentally debased. The worker, therefore, feels himself at home only during his leisure time, whereas at work he feels homeless. His work is not voluntary but imposed, *forced labour*. It is not the satisfaction of a need, but only a *means* for satisfying other needs.[11]

Indeed, whilst he works to make money for himself, the purpose of the collective enterprise of which he forms a tiny part is to transform matter into marketable commodities, for his employer. The commodities, as he well knows, will procure profits for someone whose interests conflict with his own. And the money he earns stands somewhat in the same relationship to himself as that of the idol to its maker, it is a symbol of his alienation.

The worker's wages are spent on satisfying 'wants' and 'musts' artificially created by the system, again, for the purpose of making profits for the capitalist class. To acquire these he sells his labour and in the process he and his work become, as it were, commodities too. In this sense his work is 'forced labour'; he must sell it to an employer if he is to survive. This determines his relationship to the employer. One is set against the other. They are alienated from each other as human beings.

Capitalist man is at numerous different levels 'a stranger in a strange land'. He is alienated from his work, his fellows, (with whom he has to compete) and society.

> A direct consequence of the alienation of man from the product of his labour, from his life activity and from his species-life is that *man is alienated* from other *men*. When man confronts himself he also confronts *other* men. What is true of man's relationship to his work, to the product of his work and to himself, is also true of his relationship to other men, to their labour and to the objects of their labour.
>
> In general, the statement that man is alienated from his species-life, is that *man is alienated* from other *men*. When and that each of the others is likewise alienated from human life.[12]

The worker is made by capitalist society into an object, a 'thing'. So too, for that matter, is the employer—and, contrary to general belief, Marx showed himself to be concerned with the alienation and dehumanisation of the employer as well as of the worker. Each is equally debased by capitalism: 'Prostitution is only a *specific* expression of the *general* prostitution of the *labourer*, and since it is a relationship in which not the prostitute alone, but also the one who prostitutes, fall—and the latter's abomination is still greater—the capitalist, etc., also comes under this head.'

As capitalism develops so alienation grows. Automation aggravates rather than reduces alienation: 'Rising wages presuppose, and also bring about, the accumulation of capital; thus they increasingly alienate the product of labour from the worker. Likewise, the division of labour makes him increasingly one-sided and dependent, and introduces competition not only from other men but also from machines. Since the worker has been reduced to a machine, the machine can compete with him.'[13]

The unemployed British worker, the semi-skilled and unskilled people of the black ghettoes of America who are surplus to the requirements of automated industry, both have reason to know what competition with the machine can mean in practice.

Alienation in its manifold forms embraces the whole of developed, technological, industrial capitalist society. It has reached a point where, as Marcuse has shown in his *One Dimensional Man*, the system has become one of universal saleability, of universal marketing, touching every aspect of human life. Man is increasingly estranged from his own creative powers, diminished in his humanity.

The alienated character of the worker's labour 'appears in the fact that it is not his work but work for someone else, that in work he does not belong to himself but to another person.'[14]

The 'other person', the capitalist, is alienated from his fellow capitalists by the competitive system of which he is both an agent and a victim. Instead of having a human relationship with 'his' work-people he is thrown into an antagonistic relationship with them. The profits he derives from their labour are subject to trends over which he has little control. He spends his money on maintaining a style and way of life predetermined by others—ranging from fellow capitalists in search of new marketable products to advertising agents and professional trend setters—similarly in search of profits.

Marx is concerned with the emancipation of the whole of alienated mankind:

> It follows, from the relation between alienated labour and private property, that the emancipation of society from private property, from servitude, takes the political form of the *emancipation of the working class*, not in the sense that only the latter's emancipation is involved, but because this emancipation includes the emancipation of humanity as a whole. For all human servitude is involved in the relation of the worker to production, and all the types of servitude are only modifications or consequences of this relation.[15]

Socialists have always contended that under capitalism production is not for use but for profit. In our technological industrial society commodities are increasingly manufactured with the avowed intention of their having only a limited period of use. Planned obsolescence ensures a never-ending process of profitable production—and largely useless labour— in which authentic human need has been sacrificed to production for profit. Public taste is manipulated to a point where genuine use and potential durability are of secondary importance and where the greatest effort and ingenuity are given to persuading people that they should have, and like, what industry has manufactured for them.

Prophetically, Marx held that as capitalist man became increasingly alienated so ever-greater emphasis would be given to eating, drinking and procreating, to man's dwelling and his personal adornment. As he was made less truly human by society so capitalist man would become increasingly pre-occupied with those aspects of his life which he shares with the animals.

One has only to scan the advertisements in any glossy magazine today to see the truth of this, but it is Marx who tells us perceptively that even this is a somewhat pitiful manifestation of the individual's attempt to retain something he can call his own.

> We arrive at the result that man (the worker) feels himself to be freely active only in his animal functions—eating, drinking and procreating, or at most also in his dwelling and in personal adornment—while in his human functions he is reduced to an animal. The animal becomes human and the human becomes animal.
>
> Eating, drinking and procreating are of course also genuine human functions. But abstractly considered, apart from the environment of human activities, and turned into final and sole ends, they are animal functions.[16]

Estranged from himself as he is by his work, which occupies so much of his time, thought, and nervous energy, and by the system, man feels himself to be in control of his own situation, able to determine it for himself, only when he is engaged in forms of private activity which he supposes are uniquely his own. So more and more he turns to sex, clothes, food and the accumulation of gadgets for his home as forms of 'non-alienated' activity. But even as he does so the system seizes upon these as new sources of profit.

Indeed, capitalism, as Herbert Marcuse emphasises, is by now capable of subsuming and integrating into the system even the problems it creates—ranging from the exploitation of sex to the commercialisation of the very protest movement itself through the profitable sale of protest discs, beads, badges and the works of Che Guevara.

New forms of alienation within capitalist society are created by scientific and technological advance. Ernst Fischer, Austrian Communist leader, wrote in *The Necessity of Art: A Marxist Approach*:

> The contradiction between the findings of modern science and the backwardness of social understanding also encourages a sense of alienation. Modern knowledge about the structure of the atom, the Quantum and Relativity theories, the new science of cybernetics, have made the world an uneasy place for the man in the street—far uneasier than the discoveries of Galileo, Copernicus, and Kepler made the world for mediaeval man. . .
>
> Alienation has had a decisive influence on the arts and literature of the twentieth century. It has influenced the great writings of Kafka, the music of Schoenberg, the Surrealists, many abstract artists, the 'anti-novelists' and 'anti-dramatists'. . .
>
> The sense of total alienation veers into total despair, veers into nihilism.[17]

The tens of thousands of young people from well-to-do homes who have sought emancipation by opting out as hippies, joining communes or accepting anarchist ideas bear witness to the above. Thousands more seek a society in which man ceases to be 'a crippled monstrosity and becomes a fully developed human being'.[18]

No Christian need rush in to do battle with the Marxists over this problem of alienation. Alienation is real. Nothing would be more absurd than to try to deny its existence just because Marx and his followers have made it their special concern. In making it a subject of discussion, the Marxists have made a contribution to a better understanding of the problems of twentieth-century man. They may not have the answer but even to have men asking the right questions is of value in itself.

Marxist and Christian criticism of our technological industrial society frequently runs along similar lines. The Marxist prefers his critique to be seen as a 'scientific' rather than a moral one. The Christian's is more likely to take the form of avowedly moral protest. Looking at Marx's theory of alienation the Christian may object that although Marxism describes the mechanics, as it were, of the process it still does not explain why it should be.

To say that once the required conditions came into existence primitive man proceeded to exploit his fellows by appropriating their labour and the products of their labour still does not tell us why he should wish to do this. The 'how' is answered, but the 'why' remains in the air. For the Christian the answer to this is to be found in the nature of man—in individual man, not in society. Greed, selfishness, avarice, cruelty come into the picture at that Marxist moment of qualitative change when man seizes what is his brother's and, piling up 'treasures on earth', says 'this is mine' and in the process alienates not only other men but himself as well. The problem continues across the centuries.

Even according to Marxist thinking, alienation does not end with the ending of capitalism, and men living in the socialist part of the world are reading Marx on alienation today and recognising in it a description of their own condition. In countries ruled by Communist governments there are still inequalities. In theory, the worker in socialist society should, since he works for the State rather than for a capitalist employer, be less alienated than his brother living under capitalism. In practice, the evidence goes to show that few have any feeling of real identity with the State since, in the dictatorship of the proletariat, it has a coercive role and so stands against and outside them as a hostile, alien force. They do not feel that State enterprises, still less the State itself, are 'theirs'.

During the Stalin period the State was immensely developed and it continues to be abnormally strong. There is a vast bureaucracy. So decisions are still made by officials and bureaucrats while the people remain mere recipients, still manipulated.

It is good Marxism-Leninism to acknowledge that where there is a State there is coercion. Where the State is openly and avowedly dictatorial the alienation may weigh less heavily on some than on others, but it is nonetheless real. Contrary to Marxist-Leninist expectations the State shows little sign as yet of 'withering away'. Only under Communism, Marx claimed, would the problem of alienation be resolved, the contradictions be reconciled:

> *Communism* as the *positive* transcendence of *private property*, as human *self-estrangement*, and therefore as the real *appropriation of the human* essence by and for man; communism therefore as the complete return of man to himself as a

social (i.e. human) being. . . This communism is . . . the
genuine resolution of the conflict between man and nature
and between man and man . . . between freedom and
necessity, between the individual and the species. Communism is the riddle of history solved. . .[19]

The dictatorship of the proletariat is likely to last for a long
time yet and the 'pure' Communist society of which Marx
writes is far, far away over the distant horizon. The problem
of alienation is likely to continue to be an important feature
of the human predicament and to remain common to socialist
and capitalist man alike.

This is not to say that Christians cannot accept that man
may evolve towards a society in which the problem of
alienation is resolved; still less that they should not work and
fight for it. Teilhard de Chardin believed this to be part of
the future of man. Pope Paul VI in his encyclical *Populorum
Progressio* holds out a vision of a world that is 'truly human'
because it is 'truly Christian'. It would, he says, be a world
where all men live in dignity. Alienated man does not live in
dignity. His humanity is diminished by his alienation. It is
diminished, too, each time he diminishes the stature of his
brother whether it be by greed, selfishness or exploitation.

For the Communist it may be enough to say that the
circumstances produce the alienation. The Christian in
dialogue with him wants to know what brings about those
circumstances, and finds the answer in man's nature, in sin.
At this point the differences become fundamental.

While he was still Archbishop Montini of Milan, Pope
Paul wrote: 'When a society is composed of living men, that
is, men living by the grace of God, and living truly as
Christians, it can be hoped that in the world's tomorrow

there will be no more poor who suffer hunger, no more injustice that has no repair, no more misery without remedy. Christian society will know also how to remove these consequences of sin.'[20]

A Christian world would be one of love and peace, and justice as well, for without justice there can be no peace. If a vision is to become a reality, it must be worked for and struggled for too. About that Christians and Marxists can most certainly agree.

FURTHER READING
Chapter 8

Isaac Deutscher, *The Prophet Armed: Trotsky 1879–1921*, London: Oxford University Press, 1954.

Isaac Deutcher, ed., *The Age of Permanent Revolution: A Trotsky Anthology*, New York: Dell, 1964.

Sidney Finkelstein, *Existentialism and Alienation in American Literature*, New York: International Publishers, 1965.

Erich Fromm, *Marx's Concept of Man*, New York: Ungar, 1963.

Roger Garaudy, *From Anathema to Dialogue*, Introduction by Karl Rahner, London: Collins, 1967.

Giulio Girardi, *Marxism and Christianity*, Dublin: Gill, 1968.

James Klugmann, ed., *Dialogue of Christianity and Marxism*, London: Lawrence & Wishart, 1970.

Herbert Marcuse, *One Dimensional Man*, Boston: Beacon Press, 1969.

Karl Marx, *Early Writings*, edited by T. B. Bottomore, London: Watts, 1963.

Karl Marx, *Economic and Philosophic Manuscripts of 1844*, tr., Martin Milligan, Moscow: Foreign Languages Publishing House, 1969.

Karl Marx, *Selected Writings in Sociology and Social Philosophy*,
    edited by T. B. Bottomore & Maximilien Rubel, London:
    Penguin Books, 1963.
David McLellan, *Marx's Grundrisse*, London: Macmillan,
    1971.
István Mészáros, *Marx's Theory of Alienation*, London: Merlin
    Press, 1970.

NOTES

CHAPTER 1

[1] Leon Trotsky, *Where is Britain Going?*, 1926.

[2] *History of the Communist Party of the Soviet Union*, ed. A. Rothstein, Moscow: Foreign Languages Publishing House, 1960, 387.

[3] Jean-Paul Sartre, *Search for a Method*, E. tr. Hazel E. Barnes, New York: Knopf, 1967, 22.

[4] *Ibid*, 23.

CHAPTER 2

[1] London: Lawrence & Wishart; Moscow: Foreign Languages Publishing House; 1961.

[2] *The German Ideology*, London: Lawrence & Wishart, 1939, 199.

[3] *Early Writings: Contribution to the Critique of Hegel's Philosophy of Right*, translated and edited by T. B. Bottomore, London: Watts, 1963, 43-4.

[4] Frederick Engels, *Dialectics of Nature*, New York: International Publishers, 1940, 13.

[5] *Short History of the Communist Party of the Soviet Union (Bolsheviks)*, Moscow: Foreign Languages Publishing House, 1939, 113.

[6] J. Stalin, *op. cit.*, 109.

CHAPTER 3

[1] *Selected Works, II*, London: Lawrence & Wishart, 1936, 446.

[2] Tom Bell, *British Communist Party—A Short History*, London: 1937, 82.

[3] *Programme of the Communist International*, Chapter VI, part 2, London: Modern Books, 1932.

[4] *Ibid*, 61.

[5] Joseph Stalin, *Leninism, I*, Moscow-Leningrad: Co-operative Publishing Society of Foreign Workers in the U.S.S.R., 1934, 85.

[6] J. Stalin, *The October Revolution*, London: Martin Lawrence (undated), 50.

[7] *Ibid.* 128-9.

[8] See *The Proletarian Revolution and the Renegade Kautsky, Selected Works VII*, London: Lawrence & Wishart 1937, 182.

[9] V. I. Lenin, *The United States of Europe Slogan, Collected Works, XVIII*, London, 1964.

[10] *Towards Soviet Power*, London: Communist Party of Great Britain, 1934, 42.

CHAPTER 4
[1] V. I. Lenin, *Religion*, London: Little Lenin Library, c. 1932, 56.
[2] V. I. Lenin, '*Left Wing*' *Communism: An Infantile Disorder*, London: Lawrence & Wishart, 1934, 74.
[3] *Ibid.*, 68.
[4] *Ibid.*, 52.
[5] *Ibid.*, 38.
[6] V. I. Lenin: *On Socialist Ideology and Culture*, Moscow: Foreign Languages Publishing House (undated), 51.
[7] V. I. Lenin, *Religion*, 18.
[8] *Ibid.*, 19.
[9] See Daniel Cohn-Bendit, *Obsolete Communism—the Left Wing Alternative*, London: André Deutsch, 1968, 237.
[10] *Lenin on Britain*, London: Martin Lawrence, 1934, 217.
[11] *Historical Materialism: Basic Problems*, Moscow: Progress Publishers, 1968, 291.

CHAPTER 5
[1] *The British Road to Socialism: The Communist Party Programme*, 1968, 48.
[2] *Ibid.*, 48.
[3] *Ibid.*, 49–50.
[4] F. Engels in the Preface to the English edition of Karl Marx, *Capital, I*, Moscow, 1961, 6.
[5] *World Revolutionary Movement of the Working Class*, Moscow, 1967, 369–70.
[6] James Klugmann, *The Socialist Revolution*, a Communist Party publication (London, 1968), based on articles reprinted from the *Morning Star*.
[7] Joseph Stalin, Introduction to *Foundations of Leninism*, London, 1940.
[8] V. I. Lenin: '*Left Wing*' *Communism: An Infantile Disorder*, London: Martin Lawrence, 1934, 65.
[9] Lenin, *Guerrilla Warfare, Collected Works, II*, London, 1929, 213.
[10] *Selected Works, III*, London: Lawrence & Wishart, 1936, 312.
[11] *Lenin on Britain*, 1934 edition, 168.
[12] *The Programme of the Communist International*, London: Martin Lawrence, 1929, 9.
[13] *Ibid.*
[14] *Ibid.*

CHAPTER 6

[1]Frederick Engels, *The Origin of the Family, Private Property and the State*, London, 1940.

[2]Lenin, *The State and Revolution, Selected Works, VII*, London: Lawrence & Wishart, 1937, 10.

[3]*Ibid.*

[4]V. I. Lenin, *The Proletarian Revolution and the Renegade Kautsky, Collected Works, XXVIII*, 108.

[5]V. I. Lenin, *Collected Works, XXVIII*, 372.

[6]V. I. Lenin, *The State and Revolution, Selected Works, VII*, 80, 81.

[7]V. I. Lenin, *Greetings to the Hungarian Workers, Collected Works, XXIX*, London, 1966, 388.

[8]V. I. Lenin, *Collected Works, XXX*, 114.

[9]V. I. Lenin, *Collected Works, XXXI*, 44.

[10]V. I. Lenin, *Collected Works, XXX*, 115.

[11]'Korea Today', Pyongyang, No. 175, 1971.

[12]Ignace Lepp: *From Karl Marx to Jesus Christ*, London: Sheed and Ward, 1959, 142.

[13]*The Russian Revolution and Leninism or Marxism?*, University of Michigan Press, 1961, 84.

[14]*Ibid.*, 102.

[15]*Ibid.*, 62.

[16]*Ibid*, 69.

[17]*Ibid.*, 71.

[18]*Ibid.*, 71-2.

[19]*Ibid.*, 78.

[20]For another Marxist viewpoint see Georg Lukács, *History and Class Consciousness*, London: Merlin Press, 272 and *passim*.

CHAPTER 7

[1]Chen Po-ta, *Mao Tse-tung on the Chinese Revolution*, Peking: Foreign Languages Press, 1963, 73.

[2]*On Contradiction*, Peking: Foreign Languages Press, 1960, 10.

[3]From an editorial in *Jen-min jih-pao*, 5 April, 1956: 'On the Historical Experience of the Dictatorship of the Proletariat'.

[4]Mao Tse-tung, *On the Correct Handling of Contradictions among the People*, Peking: Foreign Languages Press, 1960, 9, 10.

[5]*Origin and Development of the Differences Between the Leadership of the C.P.S.U. and Ourselves*, Peking, 1963.

[6]Che Guevara and Mao Tse-tung, *Guerrilla Warfare*, London: Cassell, 1962, 111.

[7]*The Dialectics of Liberation*, London: Penguin Books, 1968, 161.

[8]*Ibid.*, 168.

[9]*Tricontinental*, January-February issue, 1969, Havana, Cuba.

[10]For example, in the writings of Frantz Fanon, whose book *The Wretched of the Earth* has profoundly affected the Black Power and Black Panther movements in countries of the West.

CHAPTER 8

[1]Leon Trotsky, *Their Morals and Ours*, Colombo, Ceylon: Young Socialist Publications, 1964, 34.

[2]Leon Trotsky, *The Age of Permanent Revolution: a Trotsky Anthology*, ed. Isaac Deutscher: 'The Why and Wherefore of These Trials', New York: Dell, 269.

[3]Leon Trotsky, *The Revolution Betrayed*, Colombo, Ceylon: Young Socialist Publications, 1964, 289.

[4]Leon Trotsky, *The Permanent Revolution*, Colombo, Ceylon: Young Socialist Publications, 1964, 6.

[5]See Article 92.

[6]Karl Marx, *Economic & Philosophic Manuscripts of 1844*, E. tr. Martin Milligan, Moscow: Foreign Languages Publishing House, 1959, 112.

[7]Routledge & Kegan Paul, 1968.

[8]*Marx's 'Grundrisse'*, ed. David McLellan, London: Macmillan, 1971, 152.

[9]Karl Marx, *Early Writings*, ed. and tr. T. B. Bottomore, 122, 123.

[10]See Herbert Marcuse, *Reason and Revolution*, London: Routledge & Kegan Paul, 1968, 278.

[11]Karl Marx, *Early Writings*, ed. and tr. T. B. Bottomore, 125.

[12]*Ibid.*, 129.

[13]Karl Marx, *Early Writings*, ed. and tr. T. B. Bottomore, 73.

[14]*Karl Marx: Selected Writings in Sociology & Social Philosophy*, ed. T. B. Bottomore and Maximilien Rubel, London: Penguin Books, 1965, 178.

[15]*Ibid.*, 184, 185.

[16]Karl Marx, *Early Writings: 'Alienated Labour'*, ed. and tr. T. B. Bottomore, 125.

[17]Penguin Books, 1963.

[18]Marx, *Capital, I,* Chicago: Kerr, 1906, 316.

[19]Marx, *Economic and Philosophic Manuscripts of 1844*, E. tr. Martin Milligan, 102.

[20]*Paul VI Dialogues: Reflections on God and Man*, New York: Trident Press, 1965, 129.

INDEX